BASIC – NOT BORING
SOCIAL STUDIES SKILLS

WORLD GEOGRAPHY

Grades 6–8+

Inventive Exercises to Sharpen
Skills and Raise Achievement

Series Concept & Development
by Imogene Forte & Marjorie Frank
Exercises by Leland Graham & Frankie Long

Incentive Publications

BY WORLD BOOK

About the cover:
Bound resist, or tie dye, is the most ancient known
method of fabric surface design. The brilliance of the basic
tie dye design on this cover reflects the possibilities that
emerge from the mastery of basic skills.

Illustrated by Kathleen Bullock
Cover art by Mary Patricia Deprez, dba Tye Dye Mary®
Cover design by Marta Drayton, Joe Shibley, and W. Paul Nance
Edited by Anna Quinn

ISBN 978-0-86530-371-3

World Book, Inc.
180 North LaSalle Street
Suite 900
Chicago, Illinois 60601
USA

For information about World Book and Incentive Publications products, call **1-800-967-5325,** or visit our websites at **www.worldbook.com** and **www.incentivepublications.com.**

Printed in the United States of America by Mercury Print Productions, Rochester, New York.

TABLE OF CONTENTS

CELEBRATE BASIC WORLD GEOGRAPHY SKILLS

Basic does not mean boring! There certainly is nothing dull about . . .

. . . visiting deserts and oases and icebergs and volcanoes

. . . tracking down the deepest canyon in the world

. . . wondering what's so wonderful about the world wonders

. . . figuring out how far a barrel drops over one of the world's greatest waterfalls

. . . getting to know some of the world's most interesting cities

. . . telling the difference between Gabon, Gambia, and Ghana

. . . planning a whirlwind trip around the world

. . . adventuring around the deserts and jungles of Africa

. . . becoming an expert on the waterways of the world

. . . discovering that polar bears and penguins may not live where you thought

. . . telling what time it is in Sri Lanka, Togo, or Fiji

The idea of celebrating the basics is just what it sounds like—enjoying and improving social studies skills. The pages that follow are full of exercises for students that will help to review and strengthen specific, basic skills in the content area of social studies. This is not just another ordinary "fill-in-the-blanks" way to learn. The activities will put students to work applying a rich variety of the most important facts and knowledge about many aspects of world geography while they enjoy fun and challenging activities about oceans and continents, countries and landmarks, cities and climates.

The pages in this book can be used in many ways . . .

- for individual students to sharpen a particular skill
- with a small group needing to relearn or strengthen a skill
- as an instructional tool for teaching a skill to any size group
- by students working on their own
- by students working under the direction of an adult

Each page may be used to introduce a new skill, to reinforce a skill, or to assess a student's performance of a skill. And, there's more than just the great student activities! You'll also find a hearty appendix of resources helpful for students and teachers—including a ready-to-use test for assessment of these world geography content skills.

As students take on the challenges of these adventures with spaces and places and wonders around the world, they will grow in their mastery of basic skills and will enjoy learning to the fullest. And as you watch them check off the basic world geography skills and knowledge they've strengthened, you can celebrate with them!

SKILLS CHECKLIST FOR WORLD GEOGRAPHY

✔	SKILL	PAGE(S)
	List and define the geographic features used to describe a region	10, 14-27
	Identify and locate the world's continents and oceans	12-13
	Locate and describe the earth's hemispheres	13
	Identify and locate the 8 major geographic regions of the world	14, 15
	Identify the continents and countries in each of the 8 major world regions	14-27
	Determine the main geographic features of Latin America	16, 17
	Determine the main geographic features of the U.S. and Canada	18
	Determine the main geographic features of Western Europe	19
	Determine the main geographic features of Russia & Eastern Europe	20, 21, 22
	Determine the main geographic features of the Middle East & North Africa	23, 24
	Determine the main geographic features of Sub-Saharan Africa	24
	Determine the main geographic features of Southern & Eastern Asia	25
	Determine the main geographic features of the Pacific Region	26
	Locate and describe the arctic and antarctic regions	27
	Identify resources and products associated with specific countries and regions	28
	Compare sizes and populations of regions and countries	29
	Identify, locate, and compare major cities of the world	30, 42
	Identify, describe, and illustrate major landforms of the world	31, 32, 33, 35
	Identify, describe, and locate the world's most important bodies of water	32, 33, 34
	Identify, describe, and locate major geographic features of the world	32, 33, 34, 35, 37
	Identify, describe, and locate major cultural and man-made features of the world	32, 33, 38
	Describe and locate the world's major climate patterns and zones	36, 37
	Identify and locate the states of the U.S. and provinces & territories of Canada	39
	Identify and locate capital cities and other major cities of U.S. and Canada	42
	Identify and describe features of the main geographical regions of the U.S.	40, 41
	Define latitude and longitude; describe features of latitudinal zones	43, 44
	Locate places on a map or globe using latitude and longitude	43, 44
	Use map scales to find distances	45
	Use map keys and symbols to find information	46
	Identify and find information on different kinds of maps	13, 14, 16-26, 36, 43-48
	Locate places on a variety of maps	13, 14, 16-26, 43-48

WORLD GEOGRAPHY

Skills Exercises

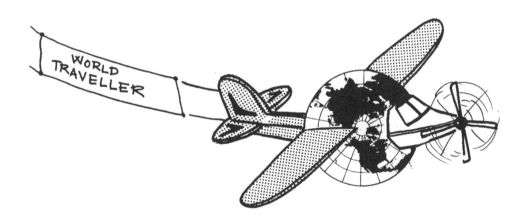

GEOGRAPHICALLY SPEAKING

Would you rather eat a *desert* or a *dessert*? Could you *ford* a *fjord*? Where is there a *cape* that you cannot wear? Is every *strait straight*? Can you tell a *mesa* from a *butte* from a *plateau*? The italicized words are all geographic features. You cannot answer the questions about them unless you know what they mean. Find out how much you really know about geographical features of the world.

I. Look at each numbered feature on the map on the next page (page 11).
    Write the correct label by each number in the list below the map.

* archipelago	butte	* sea	hill	plain
* lake	* peak	dune	* waterfall	plateau
* mountain range	cliff	* gulf	island	coral reef
atoll	* desert	fjord	lagoon	sound
* bay	canyon	* strait	mesa	prairie
jungle	* river	foothills	mountain	iceberg
* ocean	tundra	* isthmus	channel	swamp
beach	* glacier	harbor or port	mouth	valley
* cape	delta	* volcano	peninsula	

II. Next, become more familiar with some of these features while you practice finding them in the world. Use your textbook, maps, a globe, an encyclopedia, an atlas, or other references to find examples of the 16 features that are starred above. Here's how to do it:

1. Divide a piece of paper into sixteen sections, or little boxes.

2. Write one of the features at the top of each section as a bold label or title.

3. Explain or define the feature in your own words.

4. Find an example of that feature somewhere in the world and tell where it is.
   Write this information in the box.

5. Think of real examples of each geographic feature. Here's the challenge: You must find
   2 examples in each of the 8 major world regions (NO MORE THAN 2 from each):
   Anglo America; Latin America; Western Europe; Eastern Europe and Russia;
   Middle East and North Africa; Sub-Saharan Africa; Southern and Eastern Asia;
   and Pacific Region.

Use with page 11.

WORLD GEOGRAPHIC FEATURES

1. _____	12. _____	23. _____	34. _____
2. _____	13. _____	24. _____	35. _____
3. _____	14. _____	25. _____	36. _____
4. _____	15. _____	26. _____	37. _____
5. _____	16. _____	27. _____	38. _____
6. _____	17. _____	28. _____	39. _____
7. _____	18. _____	29. _____	40. _____
8. _____	19. _____	30. _____	41. _____
8. _____	20. _____	31. _____	42. _____
10. _____	21. _____	32. _____	43. _____
11. _____	22. _____	33. _____	44. _____

Name _____

THE WORLD AS I SEE IT

How do you see the world? Close your eyes. Form a picture in your mind of the map of the world. Even if you don't think you are a great artist, you can do this! Use the space below to draw a simple map of the world. (Open your eyes to do this part!) The compass rose will orient you to the directions. Include and label all continents and oceans and other major bodies of water you know. Also put your town or city on the map. Try to be accurate as to the sizes and locations. Remember, this is the world as YOU see it, so you won't be judged on your artistic ability.

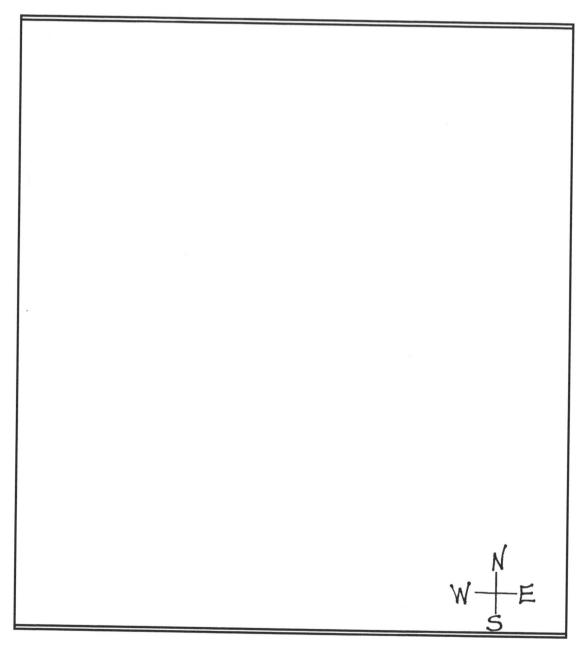

Name _____

WHICH END IS UP?

The world is divided into four imaginary halves called **hemispheres**. Each of the maps below shows a different half "up." The labels tell you which end is which; but you'll need to examine each one closely in order to answer the questions about what shows up in which end.

1. Name the continents or partial continents that are located in each hemisphere.

   Northern _____

   Southern _____

   Eastern _____

   Western _____

2. In which hemisphere(s) is the United States located?
   _____

3. Locate and label the oceans on each hemispheric map.

4. Locate and trace in red the equator on each of the hemispheric maps.

5. Which continents are **not** in the Eastern Hemisphere?
   _____

6. Which continent in the Western Hemisphere is also partly in the Northern and Southern Hemispheres?
   _____

7. Which two continents show up partially in both the Eastern and Western Hemispheres? _____
   _____

8. Which two continents fall completely in the Southern Hemisphere? _____

9. Which continent falls partly in all four hemispheres?
   _____

10. Name an ocean that is not in the Southern Hemisphere.
    _____

11. Name the continent(s) that do not extend into the Southern Hemisphere. _____

12. If you sail the entire Atlantic Ocean, what hemispheres will you touch? _____
    _____

13. Which continent lies in the Northern and Western Hemispheres and no others? _____

14. Which continent is neither in the Western nor Northern Hemisphere? _____

15. Name an ocean that is in the Eastern Hemisphere only.
    _____

Northern Hemisphere

Western Hemisphere

Eastern Hemisphere

Southern Hemisphere

Name _____

TRACKING DOWN REGIONS

You may have heard about an earthquake in Southeast Asia, a famine in Sub-Saharan Africa, a tidal wave in the Pacific Region, or a war in the Middle East. But do you really know where these regions of the world are and what countries are in them? Here's a chance to sharpen your knowledge about the world's regions. Get out your colored pencils and a good reference book with up-to-date maps. (Your geography text, an atlas, globe, or encyclopedia might help.) Track down each region and color it to match the code on the map.

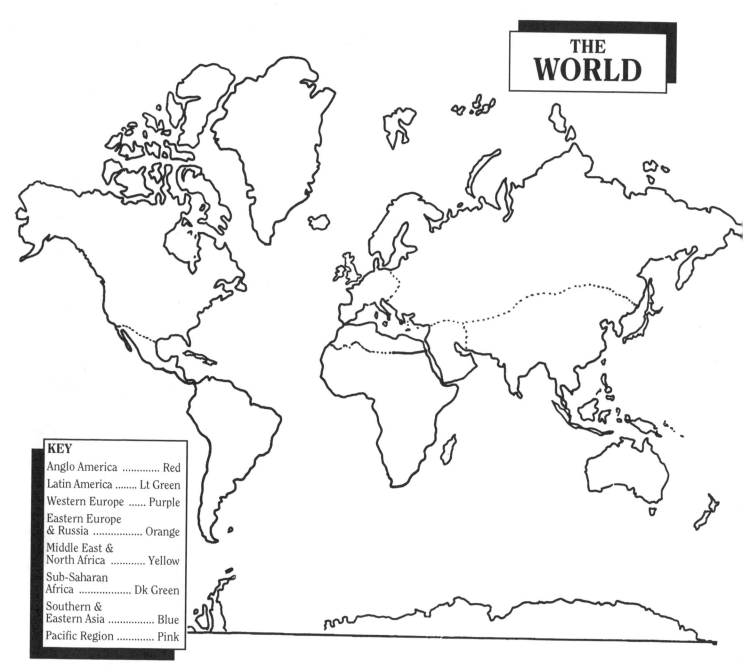

THE
WORLD

KEY

Anglo America .... Red

Latin America .... Lt Green

Western Europe ...... Purple

Eastern Europe
& Russia .... Orange

Middle East &
North Africa .... Yellow

Sub-Saharan
Africa .... Dk Green

Southern &
Eastern Asia .... Blue

Pacific Region .... Pink

Name

TRAVELING TEENS

A TV network is planning a documentary series, *Teens Travel TV Time*, which will show teenagers the major regions of the world. As the host, it is your job to plan an eight-week tour of the major regions of the world. Your budget allows you to spend one week in each region. Use the itinerary to plan your adventure in logical order. For the show, you'll need to visit at least one country in each of the major regions. Within each week's plan, be sure to include the country(ies), the cities, landmarks, and special places you plan to visit.

World Regions

Anglo America
Latin America
Western Europe
Eastern Europe & Russia
Southern & Eastern Asia
Middle East & North Africa
Sub-Saharan Africa
Pacific Region

ITINERARY

Week One:

Week Two:

Week Three:

Week Four:

Week Five:

Week Six:

Week Seven:

Week Eight:

Name _____

LATIN LANDSCAPES

The Spanish Club of Sutton Middle School is getting ready for a summer trip through Latin America. To get familiar with the land, they're creating a giant mural map of Latin America. These are some of the things they're locating and learning as they make their mural. Learn along with them by finishing the tasks and finding the answers below. Use the map on the next page (page 17) for this activity.

1. Use colored pencils to color each numbered country on the map. Label each country with its name.
2. Locate and label these bodies of water:
   Atlantic Ocean, Pacific Ocean, Panama Canal, Caribbean Sea, and Gulf of Mexico
3. Label these major mountain ranges:
   Sierra Madre Oriental, Sierra Madre Occidental, Andes Mountains
4. Find and label Mt. Aconcagua. What is its height?
5. Locate and label these rivers, then trace them on the map with blue pen or pencil:
   Magdalena, Amazon (& tributaries), Paraguay, Uruguay, Parana, Sao Francisco, Orinoco, Rio Grande.
6. Find and label Cape Horn. What country is it in? _____
7. Find and label Lake Maracaibo. What country is it in? _____
8. Place and label the pampas on the map. What are they? _____
9. What is the name of the peninsula to which Cancún is connected? _____
10. Label the large sheep-grazing area in southern Argentina. What is it called? _____
11. Which countries in South America have the highest elevation? _____

    _____

12. Do you think that Ecuador may get snow? Explain your answer. _____

    _____

13. Why was Panama chosen as the site for a canal, joining the Atlantic to the Pacific?

    _____

14. Name the Latin American countries on the equator.

    _____

    _____

15. Label the group of islands east of southern Argentina. What are they?

    _____

16. Label the islands west of Ecuador on the equator. What are they?

    _____

Use with page 17.

Use with page 16.

LATIN LANDSCAPES

EQUATOR

KEY

= Rivers

= Mountains

= Country
Borders

225   450
112   337
One
Three-Quarters of
an Inch = 450 m

Name

EDNITU TSETAS & NAACAD

These travelers from Europe are pretty mixed up about where they are on their tour of the United States and Canada. As you can see, even the names of their destinations are scrambled! Use the clue to help unscramble each geographic feature of the U.S. or Canada. Tell where they are if they find themselves . . .

NHUOSD

1. _____ . . . fishing in a large bay in northern Canada

NLEWCTERAS

2. _____ . . . canoeing on a river which separates New York from Ontario

RKYCO

3. _____ . . . hiking in a major western mountain range

SSIPPISSIMI-ISRISOMU

4. _____ . . . rafting down the longest river in North America

PEROIRUS

5. _____ . . . swimming in the largest of the Great Lakes

ACICRT

6. _____ . . . sailing on the ocean north of Canada

7. _____ . . . taking pictures of grizzlies in the state bordering the Bering

LAKASA

8. _____ . . . snorkeling in the major body of water separating Florida from Texas

LGEFOCXOIMFU

9. _____ . . . getting poison ivy in the mountain range running from Alabama to the New England states

HACPPINAALA

EANUAILT

10. _____ . . . kayaking around the islands of Alaska that extend toward Asia

LEYLHAVTDAE

11. _____ . . . getting sunburned in the lowest spot in the United States

RNAAAGI

12. _____ . . . on a boat beneath a waterfall shared by U.S. and Canada

BOIUAMCL

13. _____ . . . looking for Bigfoot near the river border between Washington and Oregon

BEQCUE

14. _____ . . . calling home from the Canadian province that stretches farthest north

15. _____ . . . skiing in the state divided into two sections by Lake Michigan

CAINGIHM

IORAANZ

16. _____ . . . standing on the edge of the Grand Canyon in this state

LRAFIOD

17. _____ . . . at a dolphin show in the state that extends the farthest south

IIWAHA

RGIEDNARO

18. _____ . . . lying on a beach in the island state

19. _____ . . . flying over the river separating U.S. from Mexico

KECNIZEMA

20. _____ . . . snowshoeing along a major river in the Northwest Territory

Name _____

WINDING THROUGH WESTERN EUROPE

Finding your way around one of the thousands of castles in Western Europe is like wandering through a maze. Hidden in this maze are the names of 25 western European countries or political entities. These include 3 small principalities, 3 political divisions of the United Kingdom, and 1 independent state which is the tiniest country in the world. Some names are found as you read from left to right. Others are in reverse or located vertically. Your task is to find each and circle the letters that make up the name of the country. The scroll below provides hints by giving you the first letter of each of the 25 names you are searching for. For example, two of the names begin with the letter A.

2—A
1—B
1—D
1—E
2—F
2—G
3—I
2—L
1—M
2—N
1—P
5—S
1—W
1—V

```
S W E D E N G L A N D F N G P
A D E N M A R K J V G I O N V
M O N A C O U M L A E N R E W
G D N A L T O C S T R L W J A
M U I G L E B F S I M A A H A
P O I E F R M N A C A N Y U N
O H N E T H E R L A N D S H D
R C Z F W T X Z I N Y T E P O
T A I H H A U Q T C R J E S R
U J R C Q Y L A T I E Q C P R
G R E E C E U E A T W L N A A
A I L W D J G L S Y L S A I Z
L S A N M A R I N O I E R N L
G G N T W E Z F R P P G F M D
T Z D E O V H U X N D T J E Q
```

FROM THE BALTIC TO THE PACIFIC

It's the largest country in the world—almost twice the size of China or the United States, covering much of Eastern Europe and most of Northern Asia. Russia covers over 6 million square miles. This giant landmass stretches from Eastern Europe to the Asian Pacific Coast.

Russia and its surrounding neighbors, formerly known as USSR (Soviet Union), were governed by a central committee located in Moscow. After the breakup of the Soviet Union, constant changes occurred in political boundaries within this region. At this time, there are fifteen independent republics as well as Russia. Even after the breakup, Russia is still the the largest country in the world. Even though political boundaries remain in flux, natural features remain the same. Use the physical map of Russia on the next page (page 21) and a current atlas to complete the following tasks and questions.

1. _____ Mountains separate European Russia from Asian Russia.

2. Trace over all of the rivers on the map in blue, and pay attention to their names.

3. Color the Cherskiy Mountains in purple; the Ural Mountains in dark green; the Caucasus Mountains in red; the Pamir Mountains in brown; the Altai Mountains in yellow; the Verkhoyansk Mountains in orange; the Sayan Mountains in light green; the Baikal Mountains in light blue; the Yablonovoy Mountains in light brown; and the Stanovoy Mountains in dark purple.

4. Locate and color the desert areas, Karakum and Kyzyl Kum, in light yellow.

5. The Kuril Islands are located in the southeast of this region. Locate and label them.

6. Two mountain peaks are labeled: Mount Elbrus in the _____ Mountains and Communism Peak in the _____ Mountains.

7. In addition to the oceans and seas labeled on the map, can you locate and label the following?

Barents Sea	Laptev Sea	Tatar Strait
Gulf of Anadyr	Gulf of Finland	Sea of Japan
East Siberian Sea	Chukchi Sea	Kara Sea

8. Find the Klyuchevskaya Volcano and the Kamchatka Peninsula where it is located. Label them both.

9. Place Moscow on the map in its proper location.

10. Name 3 countries that border Russia on the south. _____
_____

11. Name 4 countries that border Russia on the west. _____
_____

12. Find out how wide Russia is from east to west. _____

Use with page 21.

Name _____

20

Use with page 20.

FROM THE BALTIC TO THE PACIFIC

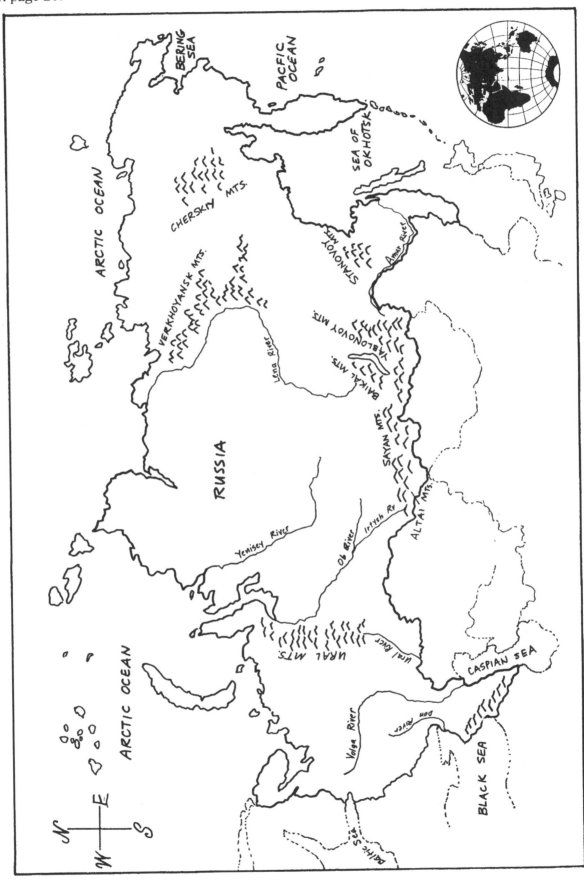

Name

LAND OF MANY CHANGES

If you learned the countries of Eastern Europe a few years ago, you'll need to start over! The map of Eastern Europe has developed a whole new look in recent history. With the breakup of the Soviet Union in 1991 and the unification of Germany in 1990, Eastern Europe has seen many changes in its political divisions. Independent republics that were once part of the USSR now show up as separate countries on maps. Changes in communist power in Eastern Europe also led to new divisions in the countries that were once Czechoslovakia and Yugoslavia. So, pay close attention to the map below. Answer these questions to brush up on your knowledge about what's where in Eastern Europe.

1. What Eastern European countries border the Ionian Sea?

2. Name the Eastern European countries bordering the Adriatic Sea.

3. Name the Eastern European countries bordering the Baltic Sea.

4. What sea is bordered by Romania and Bulgaria?

5. What 2 countries make up the former Czechoslovakia?

6. Name a country that touches the northern border of Ukraine.

7. What countries border Greece on the north?

8. Is Austria located between Hungary and Germany or Hungary and Poland?

9. Name a small country south of Ukraine that does not touch the Black Sea.

10. Name the new countries that make up the former Yugoslavia.

11. What sea borders Greece on the west?

12. Does Estonia touch the Baltic Sea?

Al=Albania	**E**=Estonia	**P**=Poland
Au=Austria	**G**=Greece	**R**=Romania
B=Belarus	**H**=Hungary	**T**=Turkey
B-H=Bosnia and Herzegovina	**L**=Latvia	**Se**=Serbia
	Li=Lithuania	**Sl**=Slovakia
Bul=Bulgaria	**M**=Montenegro	**S**=Solovenia
C=Croatia	**Ma**=Macedonia	**U**=Ukraine
CR=Czech Republic	**Mo**=Moldova	

Name

22

OF DESERTS & OASES

A land of camels . . . oases . . . deserts . . . oil . . . war . . . tradition . . . religion . . . mystery. These images may often come to mind when you think of the Middle East and Northern Africa. The beautiful deserts of this region stretch from Turkey to Tunisia, and from Morocco to Iran. This is one of the world's most important crossroads, spanning two continents (Africa and Asia). It has a rich history that extends back thousands of years. Solve this puzzle to refresh your knowledge about some of the geographic and political features of this area. If you need help, consult your geography text, an atlas, or your encyclopedia.

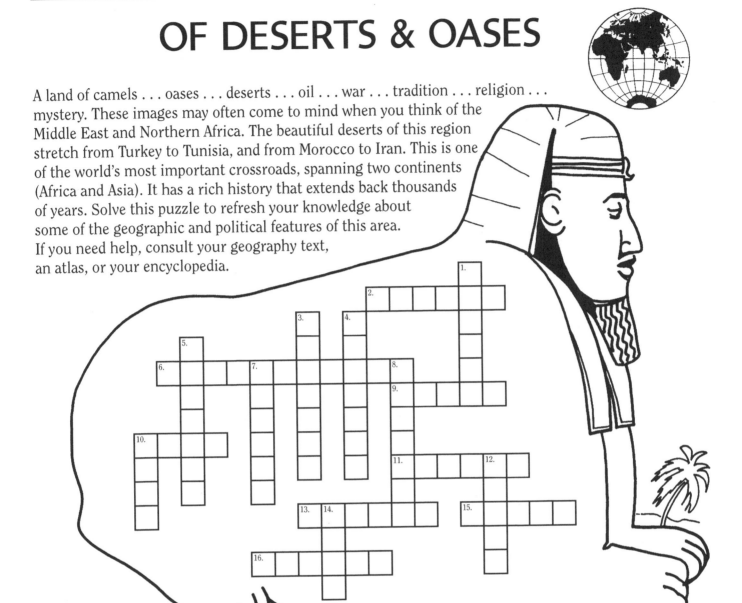

ACROSS

2 Island country in the Mediterranean Sea
6 Largest country in the Middle East
9 Libyan Desert is in Egypt and _____.
10 Present name for ancient land of Mesopotamia
11 Sea that borders Egypt and Saudi Arabia
13 Dead Sea separates Israel from _____.
15 Country at western end of Fertile Crescent
16 Country at head of the Persian Gulf

DOWN

1 Middle eastern nation in both Asia and Europe
3 Country with both an Atlantic and Mediterranean coast
4 Country north of Israel
5 Island nation in the Persian Gulf
7 Homeland for people of Jewish faith
8 Tell Atlas Mountains are located in____.
10 Country south of Caspian Sea
12 Longest river cuts through this country
14 Arabian Sea is southeast of _____.

Name

Copyright ©1997 by Incentive Publications, Inc., Nashville, TN.

AN AFRICAN ADVENTURE

For a long time, Africa was called "The Dark Continent," probably because it was far away, largely unexplored, full of scorching deserts, deep, dense tropical forests, and vast grasslands—and very mysterious. Serena Sahara, modern-day explorer, is one of many frequent visitors to Africa these days. She's just returned from a trip to Africa and is telling her friends about a part of each week's adventures. Match each of her descriptions with the letter on the map that shows the location of that place, and name the country where she is. (In some cases, there is more than one possible country; just choose one.) You'll need a good atlas to help you.

WEEK

1. I watched the flooding along the mouth of the Nile River.

2. We took a canoe through the heart of the Congo River Basin.

3. I stood at the base of Mt. Kilimanjaro.

4. I caught a boat ride on the world's largest lake, Lake Victoria.

5. I hiked through a section of the Great Rift Valley.

6. We got caught in a sandstorm on the Sahara Desert.

7. We visited the dry grasslands of the Sahel.

8. I sailed along the Gulf of Guinea.

9. I flew over to the Island of Madagascar in a helicopter.

10. Our group relaxed and swam in the Mediterranean Sea.

11. We visited bushmen tracking animals in the great Kalahari Desert.

12. We did some climbing in the Atlas Mountains.

13. I watched a sunrise over the Indian Ocean from the Somali Peninsula.

14. I saw magnificent large animals on a safari on the savanna.

15. I had a great shopping trip in Cape Town on the Cape of Good Hope.

16. I considered trying to swim the Mozambique Channel. (Decided not to!)

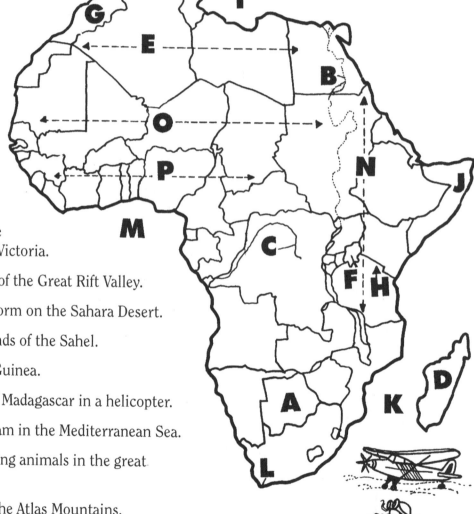

Name

ASIA, A NATURAL PATCHWORK

Over 17 million square miles it covers! And it is home to close to 500 million people! Asia is not only the largest continent but also one of the most diverse—a patchwork of natural geographic features. The sentences below include a sampling of Asia's geographic diversity.

I. On the back of this page, write the name of an Asian country for each of these letters:

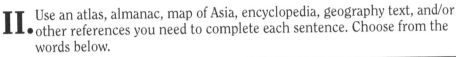

C I L M P N S

T A J B V R

II. Use an atlas, almanac, map of Asia, encyclopedia, geography text, and/or other references you need to complete each sentence. Choose from the words below.

Lake Baikal	Mt. McKinley	grasslands	Mt. Everest
Chang Jiang	easterlies	Gobi	Philippines
rain forest	Lake Victoria	Indian	Korea
paddies	taiga	subcontinent	Australia
K-2	Mt. Etna	Pamir Knot	Thailand
El Niño	Continental	Himalaya	India
Mohave	Divide	monsoons	
Sahara	Ural	Arctic tundra	

1. Asia boasts the highest point in the world—at the peak of
   _____ .

2. Seasonal winds that bring large amounts of rainfall to Asia's coastland are known as the _____ .

3. An area in central Asia where several great mountain ranges come together is known as _____ .

4. The longest river in Asia, the _____ , flows from the Plateau of Tibet into the East China Sea.

5. Stretching across most of Mongolia is the _____ , the largest desert in Asia and the third largest desert in the world.

6. Rice, one of Asia's most important crops, grows in flooded fields called
   _____ .

7. _____ , in central Siberia, is by far the deepest lake on Earth.

8. The border between Nepal and Tibet (Region of China) is formed by the _____ mountains.

9. In northern Asia, there is a vast area of permanently frozen subsoil called the _____

10. The climate of southeast Asia is tropical. Because of the heavy rains there, much of the land is covered by _____ .

11. The world's largest peninsula is _____ .

12. _____ is an example of an Asian archipelago.

Name _____

Basic Skills/World Geography 6-8+

LAND DOWN UNDER

Down under what? The land or lands "down under" refer to land that is totally south of the equator—a region in the south Pacific Ocean that is often referred to as "the Pacific Region." This region includes two continents and thousands of islands with countries that have names like Nauru, Fiji, and Tonga. It's loaded with atolls and coral reefs, palm trees and icebergs. It is an interesting combination of tropical paradise and frozen ice. To review what you know about this region (and maybe learn some new things), read each descriptive phrase in the phrase bank below and decide which part of the region it describes: Australia/New Zealand, Antarctica, or Oceania (the many island countries). Write each phrase in the correct box below. (Some phrases may fit in more than one box.)

PHRASE BANK

Interior is a desert called the outback

Mostly subtropical climate

Land of glaciers

Mostly dry except for the outer rims

Missionaries promoted European settlement

Colonized by British convicts

All but 2% of land covered with ice

Comprised of three major island groups

Generally has a polar ice cap climate

Discovery of gold sped settlement

Underwater wonderland called Great Barrier Reef

Polynesia, Micronesia, Melanesia

Known for many volcanoes

World's smallest continent

Tahiti, Easter Island, Figi, and Papua New Guinea

Remained undiscovered until about 1800

Center of literature, film, and music

Scene of bloody fighting in World War II

Has no permanent settlements

Islands made of coral

Exploration undertaken during late 1800s

Early societies based on fishing lifestyles

Loaded with icebergs and glaciers

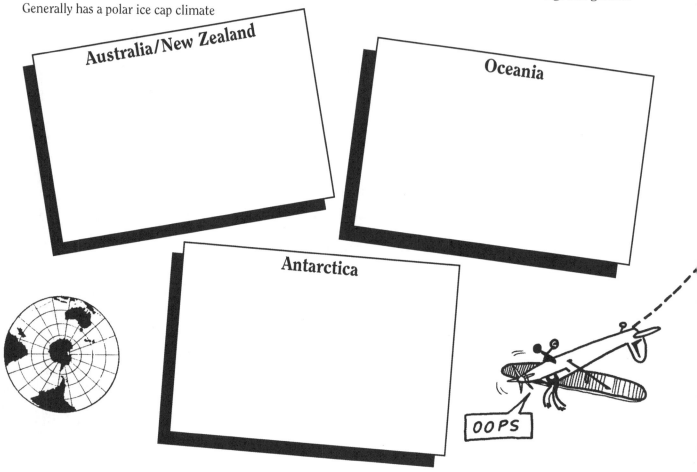

Australia/New Zealand

Oceania

Antarctica

OOPS

Name

FROM POLAR BEARS TO PENGUINS

How many polar bears summer at the South Pole? Does Santa Claus have penguins for pets? If you have to think about either one of these questions, you probably are not sure about the similarities and differences of the northern and southern polar regions of the earth. The northern polar region consists of all the area north of the Arctic Circle. The southern polar region includes all of the area south of the Antarctic Circle.

Most people think these two regions are just alike. Actually, there are some major differences in the physical characteristics of these two regions. Your job is to do some research on these two areas and find information that compares and contrasts them. When you're finished, you'll know the answers to the polar bears and penguin questions. You'll also know more about the comparison of the North Pole and South Pole than most people!

Using the cue words in the left column, complete the columns for the Arctic and Antarctic regions. If you find nothing for a category, write "none."

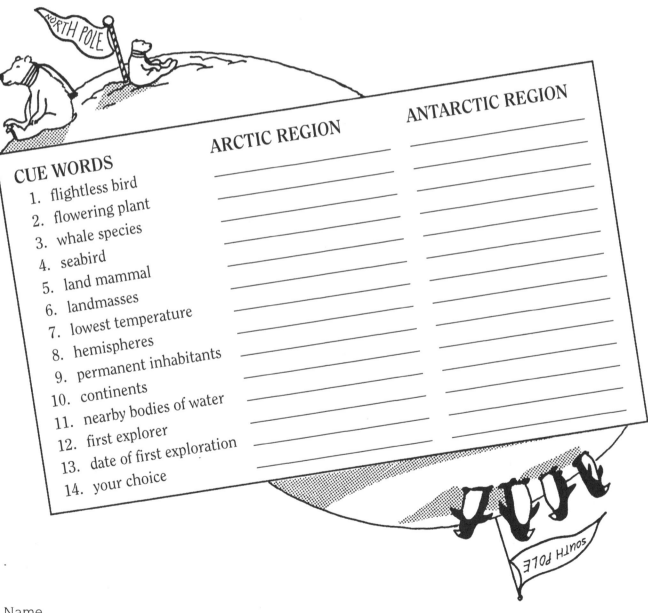

CUE WORDS

1. flightless bird
2. flowering plant
3. whale species
4. seabird
5. land mammal
6. landmasses
7. lowest temperature
8. hemispheres
9. permanent inhabitants
10. continents
11. nearby bodies of water
12. first explorer
13. date of first exploration
14. your choice

ARCTIC REGION

ANTARCTIC REGION

Name

NATURALLY RICH

The land of the world is filled with or produces some amazing riches . . . everything from rubies to diamonds to coffee to potatoes. These are the things that feed and clothe people and supply them with materials for manufacturing all kinds of supplies. This chart shows where some of the riches of the world are located. Use it to answer the following questions.

LEADERS IN WORLD RESOURCES

Agricultural Resource	1st in World	2nd in World	3rd in World	4th in World	Mineral Resource	1st in World	2nd in World	3rd in World	4th in World
WHEAT	China	U.S.	India	Russia	CRUDE OIL	Saudi Arabia	Russia	U.S.	Iran
RICE	China	India	Indonesia	Bangladesh	COAL	China	U.S.	Russia	Germany
CORN	U.S.	China	Brazil	Mexico	NATURAL GAS	Russia	U.S.	Canada	Netherlands
COFFEE	Brazil	Colombia	Indonesia	Mexico	IRON ORE	Brazil	Australia	China	Russia
TOBACCO	China	U.S.	Brazil	India	ZINC	Canada	Australia	China	Peru
COTTON	China	U.S.	India	Pakistan	ALUMINUM	U.S.	Russia	Canada	Australia
CATTLE	Brazil	U.S.	China	Argentina	GOLD	South Africa	U.S.	Australia	China
FISH	China	Japan	Peru	Chile	COPPER	Chile	U.S.	Canada	Russia
POTATOES	China	Russia	Poland	U.S.	DIAMONDS	Australia	Botswana	Russia	Zaire

1. Which 3 countries show up the most often on the chart? _____

   _____

2. What top diamond producers are in Africa? _____

   _____

3. What South American country is a top producer of cattle, corn, and iron ore? _____

4. For what products does the U.S. lead the world in production? _____

   _____

5. What are China's particular riches? _____

   _____

6. What are Russia's particular riches? _____

   _____

7. What South American countries are top cattle producers? _____

   _____

8. What top iron ore producers are not in Asia? _____

   _____

9. What top oil producers are not in the Middle East? _____

   _____

10. What product's top 5 producers are in Asia? _____

   _____

Name _____

HERE WE GROW AGAIN!

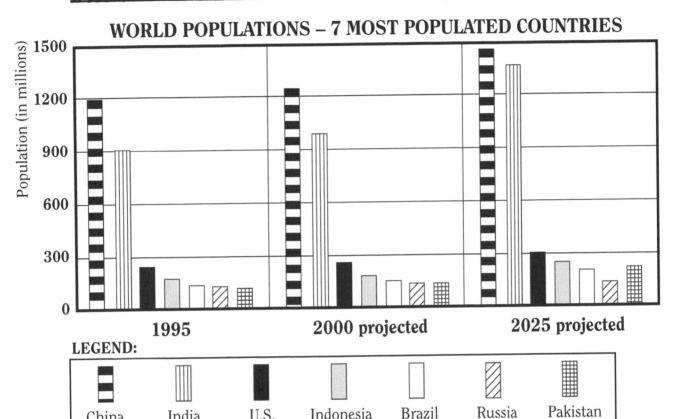

WORLD POPULATIONS – 7 MOST POPULATED COUNTRIES

LEGEND:

China | India | U.S. | Indonesia | Brazil | Russia | Pakistan

Use the information above to answer the following questions:

1. Which country has the smallest projected growth from 1995 to 2025? _____

2. Which country has the greatest projected growth from 1995 to 2025? _____

3. Which country has the greatest projected growth from 2000 to 2025? _____

4. What was the approximate total population of these countries in 1995? _____

5. What is the approximate projected total population in 2025? _____

6. Which 2 countries will likely exceed 1 billion in population by 2025? _____
_____

7. What is the projected population for Pakistan in 2025? _____

8. Which country is projected to grow by less than 50 million from 1995 to 2025? _____

9. Which 3 countries are projected to grow by over 100 million from 1995 to 2025? _____
_____

10. Which country(ies) will likely grow by more than 50 million from 1995 to 2000? _____
_____

Name _____

MAJOR METROPOLITAN MISFITS

Brush up on your knowledge of the world's major cities. In each of the following lists, all of the cities have something in common—except for one misfit. Underline the misfit. Then tell what each group has in common. Try to do this without any reference books or other aids at first, just to see what you already know. Then use an atlas to help with the rest.

1. Sacramento/San Francisco/<u>Denver</u>/Los Angeles   ___*all of these are in California*___

2. Paris/Rome/Madrid/London/Brussels _____

3. Buenos Aires/Mexico City/Caracas/Lima _____

4. Tokyo/Beijing/Haiphong/Shanghai _____

5. Pittsburgh/Chicago/New Orleans/Toronto _____

6. Bucharest/Cairo/Khartoum/Cape Town _____

7. Rio de Janeiro/Brasilia/Sao Paulo/Montevideo _____

8. Adelaide/Auckland/Brisbane/Canberra _____

9. Vancouver/Guatemala City/La Paz/Manila _____

10. Bonn/Moscow/Caracas/Warsaw/Sophia _____

11. Bangkok/Athens/Hanoi/Singapore/Rangoon _____

12. Helsinki/Odessa/Moscow/Leningrad/Kiev _____

13. London/Dublin/Liverpool/Amsterdam/Glasgow _____

14. Ankara/San Salvador/Managua/Tegucigalpa _____

15. Tehran/Nice/Baghdad/Amman/Cairo _____

16. Dallas/Boise/Calgary/Quito/Winnepeg _____

17. New York City/Oklahoma City/Mexico City/Guatemala City _____

** *Extra Challenge*

18. Atlanta/Seoul/Miami/Moscow/Los Angeles/Barcelona _____

Name _____

WHAT IN THE WORLD?

The world is full of spectacular mountains and islands, caves and craters, canyons and deserts, straits and peninsulas. But what are they? And, where are they? Find some of the world's major landforms to finish this puzzle.

ACROSS

7. World's largest continent
9. Highest mountain in Oregon, USA
12. Large isthmus in Central America
13. Separates Great Britain from France
16. Island continent
17. Great grasslands of Africa

DOWN

1. Peninsula in Northeast Egypt bordered by Mediterranean Sea and Red Sea
2. Antarctica's highest mountain
3. Africa's largest island
4. Largest gorge in the world
5. Large desert in southern Africa
6. Country in southeast Asia that consists of more than 3000 islands
8. South America's largest rain forest
10. World's highest mountains
11. Mountains that border the Iberian peninsula
14. Mountains that form the border between Europe and Asia
15. Major mountain range in Europe

Name

Basic Skills/World Geography 6-8+ Copyright ©1997 by Incentive Publications, Inc., Nashville, TN.

RECORD BREAKERS

People are always fascinated by recordbreakers . . . the biggest (or smallest), the tallest, the deepest, the longest, the widest, the highest . . . the most or least of anything. The world is full of natural and man-made features which set records as the most or least. Many are really important to know. Others are just fun for curious minds to track down. See how many of these you already know. Then use references to find the rest.

1. The largest ocean in the world covers almost 64 million square miles. What is it?
   _____

2. The longest cave system in the world is right in the U.S. in the state of _____ .
   It is called _____ .

3. The world's tallest building is located in _____. It is called _____ .

4. The world's largest desert is the Sahara. Where is it? _____
   Approximately how much area does it cover? _____ square miles.

5. The longest glacier in the world is the Lambert-Fisher Glacier. Where is it?
   _____

6. The largest lake in the world touches the countries of Azerbaijan, Iran, Kazakhstan, Russia, and Turkmenistan. What is it? _____ .

7. The world's largest sea is _____. It is in the _____ Hemisphere.

8. Hudson Bay is the world's biggest bay. Where is it? _____

9. The coldest city in the United States is _____

10. The smallest continent in the world is _____ .

11. The world's second longest river is on the continent of _____ .

12. The largest lake in the United States is _____ , next to the state of
    _____ .

13. The highest waterfall in the world is _____ Falls in _____ .

14. The largest island in the world is _____ , located in the _____ Ocean.

15. The highest waterfall in the U.S. is in _____ National Park.

16. Is Texas the largest state in the U.S.? _____ If not, what is? _____

17. Where is the world's largest gulf? _____

18. What is the smallest state in the U.S.? _____

19. The driest city in the U.S. is in the state of _____ .

20. What is the world's smallest country?
    _____

21. The world's longest river is the on the continent of _____
    _____ .

22. New Zealand is home to the world's tallest geyser. What is its name?
    _____

23. The deepest lake in the United States is in the state of Oregon. What is it? _____

More on page 33.

Name

MORE RECORD BREAKERS

Here are more record-setting geographical and man-made features of the world to track down.
This follows page 32.

24. The inhabited place with the least rainfall in the world is in the country of _____.

25. What country(ies) is (are) on the world's largest peninsula? _____

26. The deepest lake in the world is _____ in the country of _____.

27. The longest tunnel in the world is the Seikan Tunnel. Where is it? _____
    How long is it? _____

28. The world's largest active volcano is _____ located in _____.

29. The longest suspension bridge in the U.S. is in New York City.
    What is it? _____ What water does it span? _____

30. The world's busiest airport is in _____.

31. The Great Barrier Reef is the world's longest reef. Where is it? _____

32. Everyone knows that the world's tallest mountain is Mt. Everest. What country(ies) is it
    in? _____

33. What is the world's second tallest mountain? _____ Where is it? _____

34. What is the world's longest fjord? _____

35. What is the world's least populated country? _____

36. The deepest ocean trench is in the Pacific. Its deepest point is almost 36,000 feet.
    What is it? _____

37. The city in the world with the largest population is _____.

38. Where is the world's largest marsh? _____
    What is it? _____

39. What is the highest dormant volcano in the United States? _____
    What state is it in? _____

40. The deepest depression in the world holds what body of water? What countries does it
    touch? _____ and _____.

41. The country with the longest coastline in the world is _____.

42. The world's largest country is _____.

43. The most populated U.S. city is _____.

44. The world's busiest seaport is in Europe.
    Where is it? _____

45. The oldest city in the U.S. is in Florida.
    What is it? _____
    How old is it? _____

46. Just for fun: Can you find the U.S. city with the
    longest name? _____

Name _____

WATER WORLD

You're off on adventures to navigate some of the world's great waters. Where are you, if you are . . .

1. . . . exploring a large, cold ocean north of Norway?

2. . . . enjoying the warm waters east of India and west of Muanmar (Burma)?

3. . . . caught in a storm east of Italy and west of Croatia?

4. . . . wind surfing the narrow water between the British Isles and Europe?

5. . . . entering the body of water that separates Japan from Asia?

6. . . . on the deck gazing at Iran, with Saudi Arabia at your back?

7. . . . paddling up the longest river in the Western Hemisphere?

8. . . . dodging icebergs between Russia and Alaska?

9. . . . cruising off the south coast of Brazil?

10. . . . about to dock at a port in Sri Lanka?

I'M ALL AT SEA!

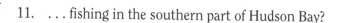

11. . . . fishing in the southern part of Hudson Bay?

12. . . . rowing across the largest crater in North America?

13. . . . crossing between Egypt and the Arabian Peninsula?

14. . . . on a cruise between Africa and Europe?

15. . . . scuba diving off your boat south of Alabama and east of Mexico?

16. . . . entering the narrow water between Malaysia and Sumatra?

17. . . . steering a freighter off the east coast of Russia?

18. . . . riding a paddleboat up the longest river in the United States?

19. . . . passing from the Atlantic Ocean into the Mediterranean Sea?

Name

NATURALLY WONDERFUL

There are many impressive things around the world. Some of the most spectacular ones are not created by humans—they are just there! These are called natural wonders. If you don't already know about these, use references to learn about their descriptions and locations so you can answer the following questions.

1. If your nose bumped into the Great Barrier Reef, what would you probably be wearing? What is the reef made of? And what country would you be in? _____

2. Serena Stoutheart went over Niagara Falls in a barrel at its highest point. How far did she fall? What two countries might she be in? _____

3. A donkey ride down into the Grand Canyon takes you how many feet down? And has you paying a visit to what state? _____

4. Why is the Dead Sea called dead? Where is it? _____

5. Where does the water come from that goes over Victoria Falls? And how far does it drop? _____

6. Climbers that make it to the top of Mt. Everest stand at what altitude? And what country(ies) are they in? _____

7. The Ross Ice Shelf is bigger than France. What is it? Where is it? And about how tall is it? _____

8. What continent and country(ies) must folks visit in order to cross the Gobi Desert? _____

9. On a cruise down the Thames River, what might Thomas and Teresa see? What country are they in? _____

10. When Patricia and Pam go off to explore the Patagonia, where are they? And what will they see? _____

11. You're on a visit to Baffin Bay. Tell why it might be called a natural wonder. Where are you when you get there? _____

12. What's so wonderful about Lake Titicaca? And where is it? _____

Name _____

THE WEATHER–CLIMATE CONNECTION

Cleo, a weather specialist, has the job of preparing a daily World Travel Weather Forecast for the Worldwide Weather News service on the internet. The cities located below are 16 of the cities she reports each day. She is constantly examining current weather in light of expected climate trends in a region. She frequently refers to a map of the world's climate zones, such as the one found on the next page (page 37.)

I. Use your colored pencils to create a color code for the map on page 37. This will help you become familiar with the world's climate patterns. On the back of the map, write some characteristics for each of the climate types, so that you get to know each type.

II. Read Cleo's forecasts below. Think about whether each forecast makes sense for the date and city given. From what the map tells you about the climate in the area where the city is located, is it likely that Cleo's forecast is correct? Write YES or NO for each city's forecast.

CLEO'S FORECAST

DATE: September 15

1. _____ **Miami, Florida:** *Cold, clear weather is expected tonight, with a frost warning for the coast.*

2. _____ **Reykjavik, Iceland:** *Snow will accumulate tomorrow, with amounts up to 4 inches.*

3. _____ **London, England:** *Tropical breezes and monsoon weather is on the way for the week.*

4. _____ **Rio de Janeiro:** *Dry, cool weather with no humidity through the weekend.*

5. _____ **Tierra del Fuego:** *Plan for a hot, muggy week, with temperatures in the 90s.*

6. _____ **Cape Town, South Africa:** *We expect heavy thunderstorms over the weekend.*

7. _____ **Baghdad, Iraq:** *Temperatures will soar today, and the 6 weeks without rain will continue.*

8. _____ **Christchurch, New Zealand:** *There has been no rain since March, and none is expected for weeks.*

9. _____ **Tokyo:** *Dry, cold snow will fall over the next 2 days—up to 2 feet is expected.*

10. _____ **Mexico City:** *The ice storms we had yesterday will continue for several days.*

11. _____ **Cairo, Egypt:** *Temperatures are over 100, and there is no precipitation in the long-range forecast.*

12. _____ **St. Petersburg, Russia:** *Monsoon season begins shortly; expect warm, humid weather and heavy storms.*

13. _____ **Denver, Colorado:** *An early winter storm could bring a few inches of snow to the Rockies this weekend.*

14. _____ **Nuuk, Greenland :** *Dry, desert breezes with temperatures in the high 90s will prevail through the week.*

15. _____ **Vancouver, BC, Canada:** *Warm sunshine, with temperatures in the 60s today and tomorrow.*

16. _____ **Helsinki, Finland:** *A hurricane watch is in effect through the night.*

Use with page 37.

Name

Use with page 36.

WORLD CLIMATE PATTERNS

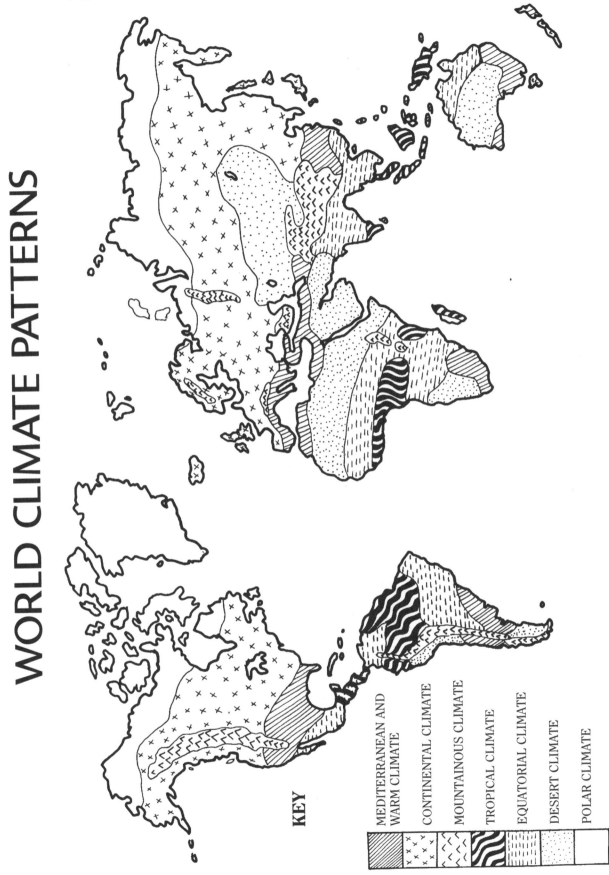

KEY

MEDITERRANEAN AND WARM CLIMATE
CONTINENTAL CLIMATE
MOUNTAINOUS CLIMATE
TROPICAL CLIMATE
EQUATORIAL CLIMATE
DESERT CLIMATE
POLAR CLIMATE

Name

WHERE IN THE WORLD?

Ivana Klue, P.I. (Private Investigator) has been hired to create a master file for a worldwide computer network that will match famous landmarks with their locations. Since her deadline is in fifteen minutes, she needs your help; otherwise, her program will crash. Use your resources to help Ivana create this file. Write the number and name of the landmark described in each phrase or sentence below.

A. A gift from France, this famous lady greets all visitors to New York City. _____

B. The world's most beautiful tomb is located in India. _____

C. One of the Seven Wonders of the World which still exists in Giza, Egypt is _____ .

D. This ancient observatory is located on a desolate plain in England. _____

E. The only man-made landmark that can be seen from the moon is _____ .

F. A famous ancient temple built over 2,000 years ago in Athens, Greece is _____ .

G. This famous bridge crosses the Thames next to the Tower of London, which was once a royal residence and later became a prison _____

H. A famous, tall monument which overlooks Paris is_____ .

I. A very famous French medieval cathedral is _____ .

J. The ancient Romans held sporting events inside this circular arena. _____

K. Hundreds of stone heads, ranging from 11 feet to 40 feet tall, line this island. _____

L. A famous Italian bell tower that is silent to prevent it from leaning further is _____ .

LANDMARK BANK
London Bridge
Easter Island
Great Pyramid
Sphinx
Mt. Rushmore
Notre Dame
Statue of Liberty
Parthenon
Panama Canal
Stonehenge
Taj Majal
Eiffel Tower
Colosseum
Leaning Tower of Pisa
Great Wall of China
Arc de Triomphe
Big Ben

Name _____

WHICH WAY USA & CANADA?

Which way do you have to look to find the name of a state, province, or territory from the USA or Canada? The names may be written up, down, or diagonally. They may read from left to right, right to left, top to bottom, or bottom to top! Use the clues to find out what state, province, or territory to locate. Then, circle its name in the scramble of letters below.

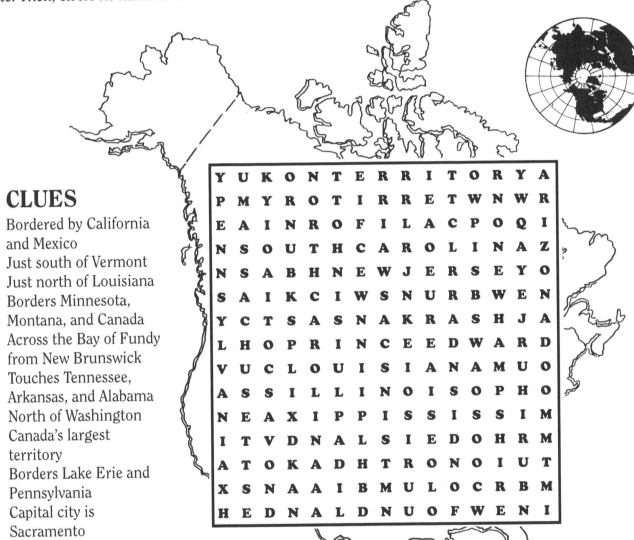

CLUES

1. Bordered by California and Mexico
2. Just south of Vermont
3. Just north of Louisiana
4. Borders Minnesota, Montana, and Canada
5. Across the Bay of Fundy from New Brunswick
6. Touches Tennessee, Arkansas, and Alabama
7. North of Washington
8. Canada's largest territory
9. Borders Lake Erie and Pennsylvania
10. Capital city is Sacramento
11. Northeast of Maine
12. South of New York
13. Shares border with Indiana and Lake Michigan
14. Touches Canada and Maine
15. Island east of New Brunswick
16. Just south of Minnesota
17. North of Delaware, shaped like a peanut
18. U.S. smallest state
19. Borders Nebraska, Oklahoma, and Colorado
20. Canada's easternmost province
21. South of North Carolina
22. North of South Carolina
23. Borders Texas and Gulf of Mexico
24. Borders Alaska and British Columbia

Name _____

Basic Skills/World Geography 6-8+

FIFTY IN FIVE

You may be planning a trip to the Northeast or have a cousin who lives in the South, but do you know exactly what those regions (and other regions in the U.S.) contain? When you're talking about or learning about the United States, it's convenient to divide it into regions—areas that share a similar past, related resources, and certain geographic features. Different maps and textbooks may divide the country in slightly different ways. The map on the next page (page 41) is one of the generally accepted ways of naming U.S. regions. It divides the fifty states into five geographic regions (Northeast, South, Pacific, Mountain, and North Central). Study the map to then complete each of the following.

1. What region do you live in? Name the states in your region.

_____

2. On vacation you ride a jet-ski in one of the two major bodies of water that border the Southern Region. Where might you be? _____
   or _____

3. You visit states having harbors along the Atlantic Ocean, the Gulf of Mexico and the Mississippi River. What region are you in?

_____

4. Cousin Cruella lives in the smallest region in area, which is _____

5. You've been to a summer camp in the region without a large water boundary. Which is it? _____

6. If you're overlooking the source of the Mississippi River, what region are you in? _____

7. You take hula lessons in the island state. Which region are you in?

_____

8. Aunt Agatha lives in one of the five states bordering the Ohio River. What two regions might she live in? _____

9. Two friends from kindergarten each moved to one of two state capitals on the Mississippi River. What are they? _____
   What regions are they in? _____

10. You've just visited Cheyenne, Boise, and Phoenix. What region have you been in? _____

11. You took a canoe trip on a large lake that splits the North Central state of

_____

12. If you live in one of the two states with four straight land boundaries, what region are you in? _____

13. Your funny Uncle Fred lives in the easternmost state in the Northeast. What is it? _____

14. Cousin Serena lives in a Pacific state that borders the Mountain region. What state might it be? _____

15. A tornado hit the northernmost state in the Southern region. Which state was it? _____

Use with page 41.

Name _____

40

Use with page 40.

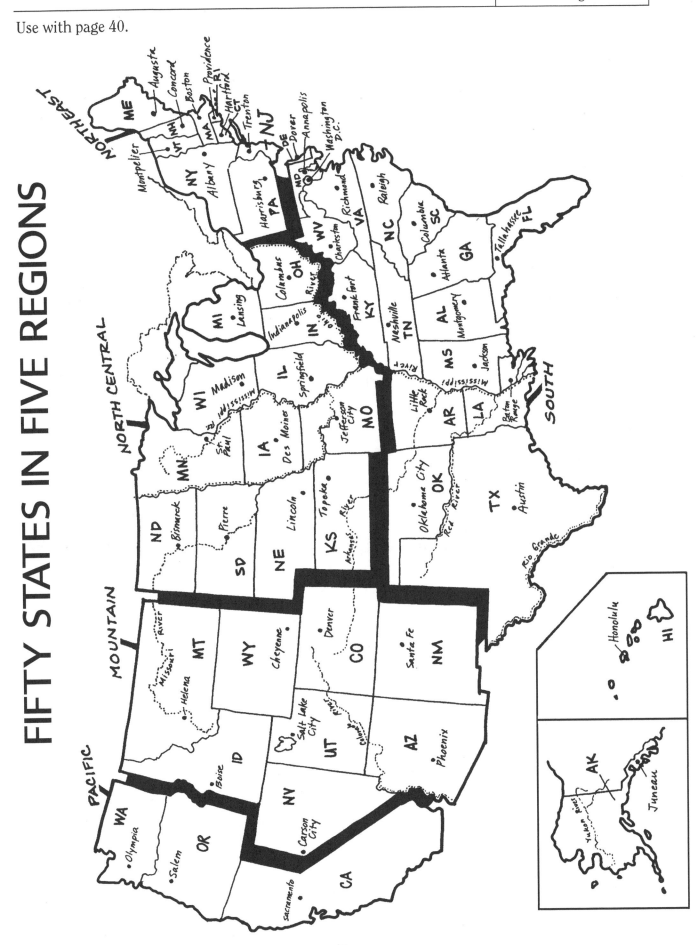

FIFTY STATES IN FIVE REGIONS

MIS-MATCHES

This city dweller had too much smog to breathe, and his matching is a little off. Which cities are correctly paired with their states, territories, or provinces? If one is, write OK. Otherwise, cross out the city names, and write in the name of a major city on this page that does match that state, province, or territory.

A.	NEW YORK	Anchorage	_____
B.	TEXAS	Boise	_____
C.	ONTARIO	Toronto	_____
D.	LOUISIANA	Tulsa	_____
E.	BRITISH COLUMBIA	Charleston	_____
F.	CALIFORNIA	San Diego	_____
G.	WASHINGTON	San Antonio	_____
H.	OKLAHOMA	Detroit	_____
I.	MICHIGAN	Montreal	_____
J.	GEORGIA	Knoxville	_____
K.	PENNSYLVANIA	New Orleans	_____

L.	TENNESSEE	Albany	_____
M.	QUEBEC	Philadelphia	_____
N.	NORTH DAKOTA	Fargo	_____
O.	SOUTH CAROLINA	Seattle	_____
P.	ALASKA	Savannah	_____
Q.	ALBERTA	Calgary	_____
R.	ALABAMA	Salt Lake City	_____
S.	MARYLAND	Baltimore	_____
T.	IDAHO	Vancouver	_____
U.	MONTANA	Helena	_____
V.	UTAH	Birmingham	_____
W.	KENTUCKY	Lexington	_____

Name _____

READING BETWEEN THE LINES

If you can read the lines (and between the lines) of latitude and longitude, you'll be able to tell where you are at any point on Earth! These lines are used to locate ships, lost hikers, and many other persons, places, and objects all over the globe. Practice using them to pinpoint exact locations.

Lines of latitude (also called parallels), tell how far north or south of the equator a place is located. On the diagram of the globe below, identify the following:

Equator
Tropic of Cancer
Tropic of Capricorn
Arctic Circle
Antarctic Circle
Low Latitudes
Middle Latitudes
High Latitudes
North Pole
South Pole

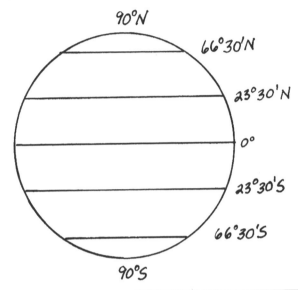

Lines of longitude (also called meridians) tell how far east or west of the prime meridian (Greenwich, England is 0°) a place is located. The international date line is located at 180° longitude. All lines of longitude meet at the poles. The diagram below shows one hemisphere. Use it to answer these:

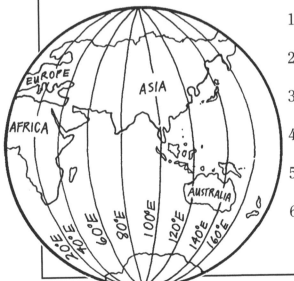

1. Trace and label the prime meridian and the international date line.
2. Approximately how far east does the continent of Africa extend? _____
3. Which of the continents pictured spreads across the most degrees of longitude? _____
4. Which longitude coordinate passes through Japan? _____
5. 40° E longitude passes through which continents? _____
6. Do any lines of longitude pass through the equator? If yes, name and explain. _____

Name _____

GET COORDINATED!

These two ace fliers are about to take a flight around the world. They are going to need a good understanding of coordinates to plan their trip. The latitude and longitude of a location are known as its coordinates. Latitude and longitude allow geographers, pilots, sailors, and others to pinpoint the exact location of any place on the globe.

The number of degrees latitude will tell you how far a location is north or south of the equator. The number of degrees of longitude will tell you how far a location is east or west of the prime meridian.

The chart gives the approximate latitudes and longitudes of ten cities where they will stop for rest, repairs, and sightseeing. Put a dot on the map to show the approximate location for each of the cities. Use the corresponding letter on the chart to label each city. Now, connect the dots with a line to show the route they will take. Don't forget to connect the last city to the first so they end up at home where they started.

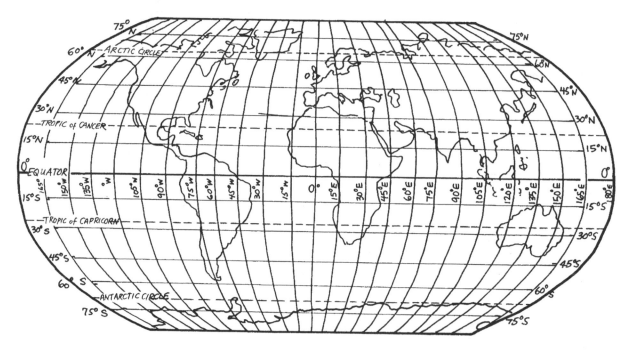

Washington, D.C., USA	38°N, 77°W	A
Mexico City, Mexico	19°N, 99°W	B
Brasilia, Brazil	15°S, 47°W	C
Cairo, Egypt	30°N, 31°E	D
Athens, Greece	38°N, 23°E	E
Rome, Italy	42°N, 12°E	F
Moscow, Russia	55°N, 37°E	G
New Delhi, India	28°N, 77°E	H
Jakarta, Indonesia	6°S, 106°E	I
Sydney, Australia	33°S, 151°E	J

Name

HOT SPRINGS AND MORE

You have chosen to attend Camp Caribou in Idaho this summer. Your camp director Patrick Hooper has sent a two-week itinerary. When you look at the itinerary, you notice that the area has many lakes, rivers, springs, mountains, national forests, and even a section of the Oregon Trail. Plan your itinerary by plotting each location on the map. Do this by answering the questions and writing on the map the number that matches each location.

1. Your adventure begins when the camp's private plane lands at Fish Haven (1) on Bear Lake (2). You are going to hike into Minnetonka Cave (3) the next day. You are in charge of giving the driver directions. Plot the route, state the direction, and state the distance.

_____

2. On Day 3, you leave camp headed north on Highway 89 (4). Follow Highway 89 until you reach Bear River (5). Your group is going to paddle the Bear River to Soda Springs (6). About how far is the trip? Will you need to spend one night on the river?

_____

3. At Soda Springs, you select your horse for the ride along the Oregon Trail (7) to Fort Hall Indian Reservation (8). On the way to Fort Hall, you need to stop for supplies. Which town does the Trail pass through?
_____ (9)

4. After your stay at Fort Hall, your next adventure is an off-road vehicle trip to Grays Lake National Wildlife Refuge Headquarters (10). After your arrival, your group hikes the loop around Grays Lake. (11) What is the approximate length of this hike? _____

5. Your group is allowed to plan your return trip to Fish Haven. On the back of this page, describe your route, tell what modes of transportation you'll use, calculate the distance, and describe three points of interest along the route. (Label the 3 points 12, 13, 14.)

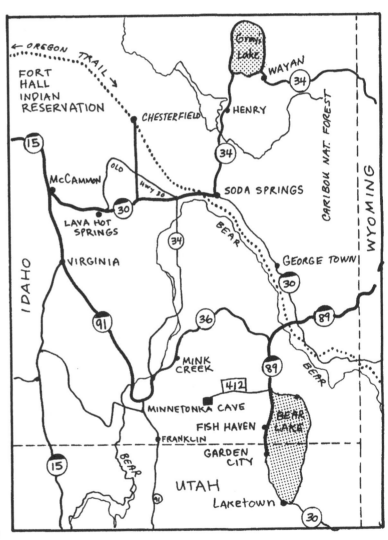

1 cm = 10 miles

Name _____

HANDS DOWN

Your crew has been sent to explore the recently discovered island of Hands Down. You have been given an aerial outline of the island. Your job assignment is to complete a thorough ground survey to create a physical map. On the map below, sketch in all of the physical features that you discover. (You decide what is found—-include such features as rivers, lakes, mountains, volcanoes, cliffs, plateaus, lagoons, canyons, caves, bays, etc.) Name the features and create a symbol key to use as a cross reference for the map. Also place a compass rose on the map to show directions.

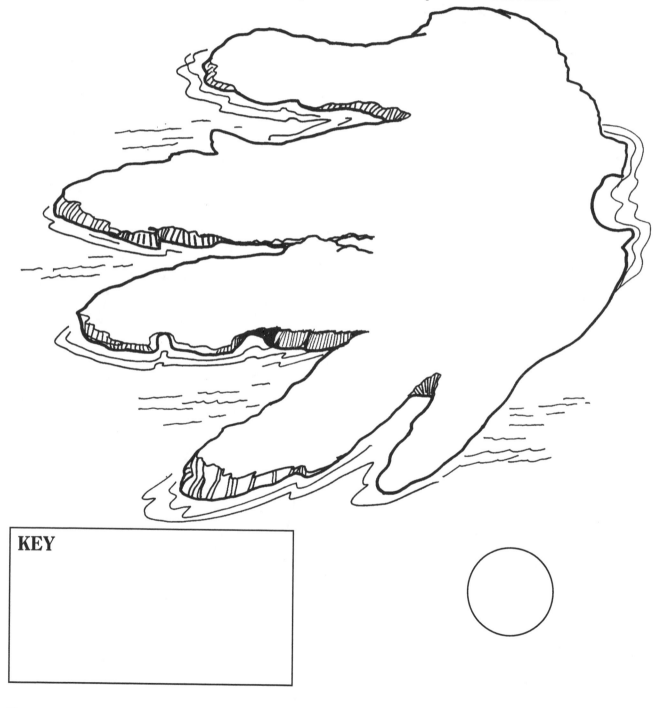

KEY

Name

A MOMENT IN TIME

Did you know for thousands of years noon was considered the time when the sun reached its highest position in the sky? Noon arrives in eastern cities first because the earth rotates toward the east. In the 1800s there were more than 50 local time zones in the United States. Stanford Fleming, a Canadian, suggested that since the earth takes 24 hours to make one rotation, the earth should be divided into 24 time zones. In 1884, a group of countries established standard time zones for the whole earth.

If you stopped time for a moment, clocks one time zone east of your location are one hour later and clocks one time zone to the west are one hour earlier than your clock. For example, if you live in Chicago and it is 8:00 A.M., is it in 9:00 A.M. in New York and 7:00 A.M. in Denver.

Imaginary vertical lines mark the boundaries of time zones. Time is measured from the prime meridian (0°). Exactly 180° in either direction from the prime meridian is the international date line, an imaginary line where each day begins. Using the time zone map provided, answer these questions.

1. How many time zones are there? _____
2. How many degrees of longitude in each time zone? _____
3. When it is noon in London, what time is it in New York City? _____
4. Your uncle sends you a ticket to visit him in Paris. Your flight leaves New York on Monday at 6:00 P.M. for a 7-hour flight. At what time and on which day do you arrive?

   _____
5. You and your uncle set out on a trip around the world! First stop . . . Copenhagen, a 2-hour flight. If you leave Paris at 10:00 A.M., what time do you arrive in Copenhagen?

   _____
6. While in Copenhagen, your uncle suggests that you call your sister who lives in Anchorage. If you want to reach her at 8:00 A.M. in Anchorage, at what time should you place your call? _____
7. Since your uncle wants you to see everything, he plans a quick trip to Algiers, Algeria. If you leave Copenhagen at 7:00 P.M., Friday, on a flight headed for Algiers, what time and day (Algiers Time) should you arrive if the flight is 4 hours? _____
8. After a few days back in Copenhagen, you head east to Bombay, India. It is 1:00 A.M. on Wednesday when you arrive in Bombay. The flight from Copenhagen was 5 hours long. What time and day did you leave Copenhagen? _____
9. From Bombay, at noon on Friday, you call your mom in Denver. What time is it for her when she answers the phone? _____
10. You leave Bombay at 5 A.M. for Hong Kong. What time is it in Hong Kong? _____
11. On to Tokyo! There, you purchased a terrific gift for your sister. Your uncle suggests that you deliver it in person to your sister in Anchorage, which is only a 7-hour flight away. You leave Tokyo at 9:00 P.M. Monday. What time do you arrive and on which day?

   _____

Use with page 48.

Name _____

Use with page 47.

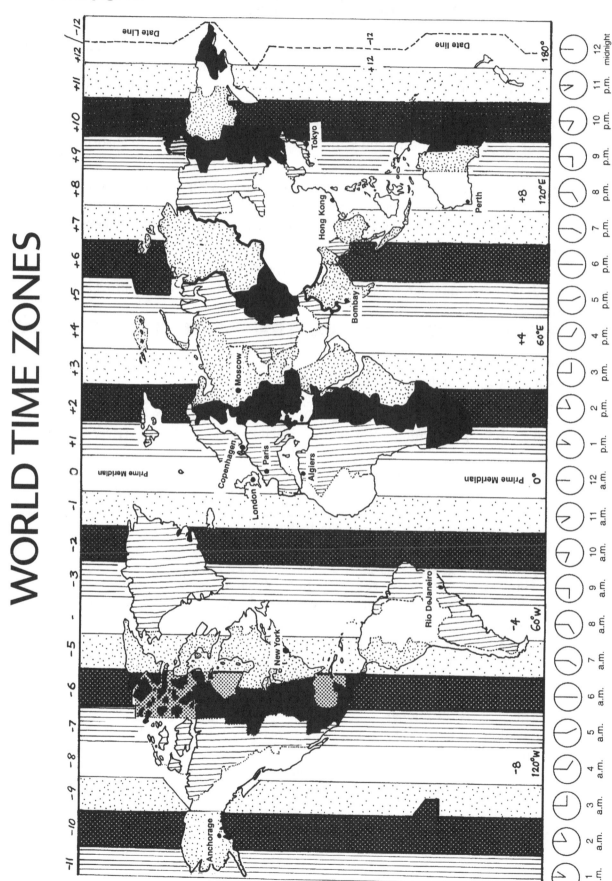

WORLD TIME ZONES

Basic Skills/World Geography 6-8+

APPENDIX

CONTENTS

GLOSSARY

GEOGRAPHIC FEATURES

archipelago: A large group or chain of islands.

atoll: A ring-shaped coral island or string of islands, surrounding a lagoon.

basin: An area of low-lying land surrounded by higher land.

bay: Part of an ocean, sea, or lake that extends into the land. A bay is usually smaller than a gulf.

beach: The gently sloping shore of an ocean or other body of water, usually covered by sand or pebbles.

butte: A small, flat-topped hill. A butte is smaller than a plateau or mesa.

canal: A waterway built to carry water for navigation or irrigation, connecting two other bodies of water.

canyon: A deep, narrow valley with steep sides.

cape: A projecting part of a coastline that extends into an ocean, sea, gulf, bay, or lake.

cliff: A high, steep face of rock or earth.

coast: Land along an ocean or sea.

dam: A wall built across a river to hold back the flowing water.

delta: Land formed at the mouth of a river by deposits of silt, sand, and pebbles.

desert: A very dry area where few plants grow.

dune: A mound, hill, or ridge of sand that is heaped up by the wind.

fjord: A deep, narrow inlet of the sea between high, steep cliffs.

foothills: A hilly area at the base of a mountain range.

glacier: A large sheet of ice that moves slowly over some land surface or down a valley.

gulf: Part of an ocean or sea that extends into the land. A gulf is usually larger than a bay.

harbor: A protected place along a shore where ships can safely anchor.

hill: A rounded, raised landform, not as high as a mountain.

island: A body of land completely surrounded by water.

isthmus: A narrow strip of land bordered by water that connects two larger bodies of land.

lagoon: A shallow body of water partly or completely enclosed within an atoll; a shallow body of sea water partly cut off from the sea by a narrow strip of land.

lake: A body of water completely surrounded by land.

mesa: A high, flat landform rising steeply above the surrounding land—smaller than a plateau, larger than a butte.

mountain: A high, rounded or pointed landform with steep sides, higher than a hill.

mountain pass: An opening or gap through a mountain range.

mountain range: A row or chain of mountains.

mouth: The place where a river empties into another body of water.

oasis: A place in the desert made fertile by a steady supply of water.

ocean: One of the earth's four largest bodies of water.

peak: The pointed top of a mountain or hill.

peninsula: A body of land nearly surrounded by water.

plain: A large area of flat or nearly flat land.

plateau: A high, flat landform that rises steeply above the surrounding land—larger than a mesa and a butte.

port: A place where ships load and unload goods.

reef: A ridge of sand, rock, or coral that lies at or near the surface of a sea.

reservoir: A natural or artificial lake used to store water.

river: A large stream of water that flows across the land and usually empties into a lake, ocean, or other river.

river basin: All the land drained by a river and its tributaries.

sea: A large body of water partly or entirely surrounded by land; another word for ocean.

source: The place where a river or stream begins.

strait: A narrow waterway or channel connecting two larger bodies of water.

timber line: An imaginary line on mountains, above which trees do not grow.

tributary: A river or stream that flows into a larger river or stream.

valley: An area of low land between hills or mountains.

volcano: An opening in the earth through which lava, rock, gases, and ash are forced out.

waterfall: A flow of water falling from a high place to a lower place.

GAZETTEER

Alps: A major European mountain system, extending in an arc from the Mediterranean coast east to the Balkan peninsula.

Amazon River: The longest river in South America and the second-longest river in the world. It flows from the Andes across Brazil into the Atlantic Ocean.

Andes Mountains: A major mountain system stretching along the west coast of South America. It is the longest mountain chain in the world.

Antarctica: The fifth-largest continent. Ice-covered, it surrounds the South Pole and lies mainly within the Antarctic Circle.

Arabian Peninsula: A large peninsula in southwestern Asia.

Arctic Ocean: The world's smallest ocean. It surrounds the North Pole and lies north of the Arctic Circle.

Asia: The largest continent, bounded on the west by Europe, on the east by the Pacific Ocean, and on the south by the Indian Ocean.

Asia Minor: A peninsula in western Asia, bordered by the Mediterranean and Black Seas. It is also known as Anatolia.

Atlantic Ocean: The second-largest ocean. It separates North America and South America from Europe and Africa.

Atlas Mountains: A mountain range extending along the northwestern coast of Africa.

Australia: The world's smallest continent, bounded by the Indian and Pacific oceans.

Balkan Peninsula: A large peninsula in southern Europe bounded by the Black, Aegean, and Adriatic Seas.

Baltic Sea: An island sea in northern Europe.

Black Sea: An inland sea between Europe and Asia.

British Isles: A group of islands off the western coast of Europe, made up of Great Britain, Ireland, and some small islands.

Caribbean Islands: Islands of the Caribbean Sea, also known as the West Indies. They are made up of the Greater Antilles, the Lesser Antilles, and the Bahamas.

Caspian Sea: The largest inland body of water in the world, located in south-central Asia.

Caucasus Mountains: A mountain range that forms part of the southern boundary between Europe and Asia.

Central America: The part of North America lying south of Mexico and north of South America.

Central Asia: A large, dry area in the central part of Asia including parts of the Soviet Union, China, and Mongolia.

Central Europe: Part of Western Europe including West Germany, Switzerland, and Austria.

Central Plateau: A large plateau in central Mexico.

Chang River: The longest river in China, flowing from Tibet east into the East China Sea. It is also known as the Chang Jiang and the Yangtze River.

Danube River: The second-longest river of Europe. It flows from southern West Germany east into the Black Sea.

East Africa: An area in Africa stretching along the east coast from Egypt south to Mozambique.

East Asia: The part of Asia that includes China, Japan, Mongolia, North Korea, South Korea, Taiwan, and Hong Kong.

Eastern Europe: The part of Europe that lies between Western Europe and the Soviet Union. It has strong political, economic, and cultural ties with the Soviet Union.

Eastern Hemisphere: The half of the world that lies east of 0° longitude and includes Europe, Asia, Africa, and Australia.

English Channel: A narrow body of water between the island of Great Britain and northwestern Europe.

Equatorial Africa: The part of Sub-Saharan Africa that lies along the equator in the central part of the continent.

Euphrates River: A river in the Middle East flowing from Turkey to Iraq, where it joins the Tigris River to empty into the Persian Gulf.

Eurasia: The large landmass on which Europe and Asia are located.

Europe: The world's sixth-largest continent. It lies between the Atlantic Ocean and Asia, from which it is separated by the Ural and Caucasus Mountains.

Fertile Crescent: A fertile crescent-shaped area of the Middle East. It was the site of several early civilizations.

Ganges River: A river in northern India and Bangladesh, flowing from the Himalayas into the Bay of Bengal.

Gibraltar: A British crown colony near the southern tip of Spain.

Gobi: A large desert in Central Asia.

Grand Canyon: A wide, deep canyon on the Colorado River in Arizona and Utah in the western part of the United States.

Great Barrier Reef: The largest barrier reef in the world, lying off the northeastern coast of Australia.

Great Lakes: Five large freshwater lakes lying along the border between Canada and the United States. They are Lake Superior, Lake Huron, Lake Michigan, Lake Erie, and Lake Ontario.

Great Rift Valley: A series of valleys in eastern Africa extending from the Red Sea south to Mozambique.

Greenland: The largest island in the world, located off the northeast coast of North America. It is part of Denmark.

Gulf Coastal Plain: The low-lying plain that borders the Gulf of Mexico.

Gulf of Mexico: An arm of the Atlantic Ocean that lies between Mexico and the Southeast United States. The Gulf Stream brings warm water from the Gulf of Mexico to the Atlantic coast of Europe.

Himalayas: The world's highest mountain system, forming part of the northern boundary of the Indian subcontinent.

Iberian Peninsula: A large peninsula of southwestern Europe that includes Spain and Portugal.

Indian Ocean: The third-largest ocean. It lies south of Asia between Australia and Africa.

International Date Line: An imaginary line running approximately along the line of longitude at 180°, in the middle of the Pacific Ocean, marking the time boundary between one day and the next.

Kalahari Desert: A large desert in southern Africa.

Lake Titicaca: The largest lake in South America and the highest navigable lake in the world. It is located in the Andes on the border of Peru and Bolivia, 16° S, 71° W.

Lake Victoria: The largest lake in Africa, located in the east-central part of the continent.

Latin America: The parts of the Western Hemisphere where Spanish and Portuguese are widely spoken. The region includes Mexico and Central America, South America, and the Caribbean Islands.

Lesser Antilles: The island, excluding the Bahamas, making up the eastern part of the West Indies, or Caribbean Islands.

Low Countries: An area in the west-central part of Western Europe that is made up of the Netherlands, Belgium, and Luxembourg.

Malay Peninsula: A long, narrow peninsula extending from Southeastern Asia into the Indian Ocean.

Mediterranean Europe: The countries of Western Europe that border the Mediterranean Sea.

Mediterranean Sea: A large, nearly landlocked arm of the Atlantic Ocean lying between Europe, Asia, and Africa.

Melanesia: One of three main divisions of the Pacific Islands. Melanesia lies south of Micronesia and west of Polynesia.

Micronesia: One of three main divisions of the Pacific islands. Micronesia is located north of Melanesia and west of Polynesia.

Middle East: The southwestern part of Asia that stretches from Turkey to Iran.

Mississippi River: The longest river in North America and the third longest river in the world. It flows south across the interior United States into the Gulf of Mexico.

Mongolia: A vast area in east-central Asia, extending from northern China to Siberia and including Inner Mongolia and the country of Mongolia.

Mount Aconcagua: The highest mountain in South America, located in the Andes Mountains between Argentina and Chile at 22,834 feet (6,960 m) at 33°S, 70°W.

Mount Everest: The highest mountain in the world. It is located in the Himalayas on the border between Nepal and Tibet at 22,108 feet (8,848m) at 33°N, 87°E.

Mount Kilimanjaro: The highest mountain in Africa, located in northern Tanzania at 19,340 feet (5,895 m) at 3°S, 37°E.

Mount McKinley: The highest mountain in North America, located in south-central Alaska at 20,320 feet (6,194 m) at 63°N, 151° W.

Nile River: The world's longest river, flowing from east-central Africa north into the Mediterranean Sea.

North Africa: Region consisting of the Muslim Countries of Africa lying along the Mediterranean coast.

North America: The world's third-largest continent, lying between the Pacific and Atlantic oceans.

North Pole: The northernmost point on the earth; the northern end of the earth's axis, at 90°N.

Glossary

North Sea: A large arm of the Atlantic Ocean, between Great Britain and mainland Europe.

Oceania: Islands of the Pacific Ocean including Polynesia, Melanesia, Micronesia, and many other islands. Australia and New Zealand are sometimes considered part of Oceania.

Pacific Ocean: The world's largest body of water, lying between Asia and Australia on the west and North America and South America on the east.

Pampas: Grass-covered plains of South America that cover much of Central Argentina and parts of Uruguay.

Panama Canal: A ship canal across the Isthmus of Panama connecting the Atlantic and Pacific Oceans.

Patagonia: The southern part of Argentina.

Persian Gulf: A body of water located between the Arabian Peninsula and Iran.

Polynesia: One of the three main island groups of Oceania in the Pacific Ocean.

Pyrenees: A mountain range in the south-western part of western Europe, extending from the western part of Western Europe, extending from the Bay of Biscay to the Mediterranean Sea.

Red Sea: A narrow sea located between the Arabian Peninsula and northeastern Africa.

Rhine River: A river in Western Europe that flows from eastern Switzerland into the North Sea.

Riviera: A narrow strip of land along the Mediterranean coasts of France, Monaco, and Italy, famous as a vacation spot.

Rocky Mountains: The high, rugged mountains that stretch along the western part of North America from Alaska south to New Mexico.

Sahara: The largest desert in the world, covering much of northern Africa.

Sahel: a dry grassland that stretches across Africa just south of the Sahara Desert.

Siberia: A vast region in the Soviet Union lying between the Ural Mountains and the Pacific Ocean. It includes most of Soviet Asia.

Sinai Peninsula: A small peninsula in northeastern Egypt, bordered by the Mediterranean Sea on the north and the Red Sea on the south. It is a bridge between Asia and Africa.

South America: The world's fourth-largest continent. It lies between the Pacific and Atlantic oceans.

South Asia: The part of Asia made up of the Indian subcontinent and nearby lands.

Southeast Asia: The part of Asia lying between South Asia and East Asia.

Southern Africa: The part of Sub-Saharan Africa that is south of East and Equatorial Africa. It is the southernmost part of the continent.

South Pole: The southernmost point of the earth; the southern end of the earth's axis, at 90°S.

St. Lawrence Seaway: The St. Lawrence River and its system of dams, locks, and canals that connect with the Gulf of St. Lawrence. This waterway allows large ships to travel between interior North America and the Atlantic Ocean.

Sub-Saharan Africa: The part of Africa lying south of the Sahara.

Tropic of Cancer: An imaginary line around the earth at latitude 23° 30′ N.

Tropic of Capricorn: An imaginary line around the earth that is at latitude 23° 30′S.

Ural Mountains: A mountain system in east-central Soviet Union, traditionally forming part of the boundary between Europe and Asia.

Vatican City: An independent state within the city of Rome. It is the world headquarters of the Roman Catholic Church; 42°N, 12°E.

Victoria Falls: A spectacular waterfall in southern Africa, on the Zambezi River between Zimbabwe and Zambia; 18°S, 26°E.

Volga River: The longest river in Europe, located in the Soviet Union. It flows from the Ural Mountains into the Caspian Sea.

West Africa: The part of Sub-Saharan Africa that makes up the southern part of the continent's northwestern "bulge."

Western Europe: The non-communist countries that make up the western part of Europe.

Western Hemisphere: The half of the world that lies west of the prime meridian and includes North America and South America.

Yucatan Peninsula: A peninsula in southeastern Mexico and northeastern Central America that juts between the Gulf of Mexico and the Caribbean Sea.

WORLD POLITICAL DIVISIONS

─── North America ───

Country	Capital
Antigua and Barbuda	St John's
Aruba	Oranjestad
Bahamas, The	Nassau
Barbados	Bridgetown
Belize	Belmopan
Bermuda	Hamilton
British Virgin Islands	Road Town
Canada	Ottawa
Cayman Islands	George Town
Costa Rica	San Jose
Cuba	Havana
Dominica	Roseau
Dominican Republic	Santo Domingo
El Salvador	San Salvador
Greenland	Godthaab
Grenada	St. George's
Guadeloupe	Basse-Terre
Guatemala	Guatemala City
Haiti	Port-au-Prince
Honduras	Tegucigalpa
Jamaica	Kingston
Martinique	Fort-de-France
Mexico	Mexico City
Montserrat	Plymouth
Netherlands Antilles	Willemstad
Nicaragua	Managua
Panama	Panama City
Puerto Rico	San Juan
Saint Kitts and Nevis	Basseterre
Saint Lucia	Castries
Saint Martin	Marigot
St. Pierre and Miquelon	St. Pierre
Saint Vincent and the Grenadines	Kingstown
Trinidad and Tobago	Port-of-Spain
Turks and Caicos Islands	Grand Turk
United States	Washington D.C.
Virgin Islands of the United States	Charlotte Amalie

─── South America ───

Country	Capital
Argentina	Buenos Aires
Bolivia	La Paz
Brazil	Brasilia
Chile	Santiago
Colombia	Bogota
Ecuador	Quito
Falkland Islands	Stanley
French Guiana	Cayenne
Guyana	Georgetown
Paraguay	Asuncion
Peru	Lima
Suriname	Paramaribo
Uruguay	Montevideo
Venezuela	Caracas

─── Europe ───

Country	Capital
Albania	Tirane
Andorra	Andorra la Vella
Armenia	Yerevan
Austria	Vienna
Azerbaijan	Baku
Belarus	Minsk
Belgium	Brussels
Bosnia and Herzegovina	Sarajevo
Bulgaria	Sofia
Croatia	Zagreb
Czech Republic	Prague
Denmark	Copenhagen
Estonia	Tallinn
Finland	Helsinki
France	Paris
Georgia	Tbilisi
Germany	Berlin
Gibraltar	Gibraltar
Greece	Athens
Hungary	Budapest
Iceland	Reykjavik
Ireland	Dublin
Italy	Rome
Latvi a	Riga
Liechtenstein	Vaduz
Lithuania	Vilnius
Luxembourg	Luxembourg
Macedonia	Skopje
Malta	Valletta
Moldova	Kishinev
Monaco	Monaco
Montenegro	Podgorica
Netherlands, The	Amsterdam
Norway	Oslo
Poland	Warsaw
Portugal	Lisbon
Romania	Bucharest
Russia	Moscow
San Marino	San Marino
Slovakia	Bratislava
Slovenia	Ljubljana
Spain	Madrid
Sweden	Stockholm
Switzerland	Bern
Ukraine	Kiev
United Kingdom	London
Vatican City	Vatican City

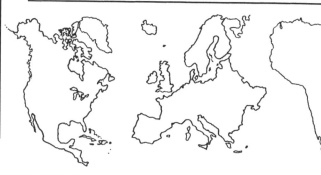

Africa

Country	Capital
Algeria	Algiers
Angola	Luanda
Benin	Porto-Novo
Botswana	Gaborone
Burkina Faso	Ouagadougou
Burundi	Bujumbura
Cameroon	Yaounde
Cape Verde	Praia
Central African Republic	Bangui
Chad	N'Djamena
Comoros	Moroni
Congo, Democratic Republic of	Kinshasa
Congo, Republic of	Brazzaville
Cote d'Ivoire	Yamoussoukro
Djibouti	Djibouti
Egypt	Cairo
Equatorial Guinea	Malabo
Eritrea	Asmara
Ethiopia	Addis Ababa
Gabon	Liberville
Gambia, The	Banjul
Ghana	Accra
Guinea	Conakry
Guinea-Bissau	Bissau
Kenya	Nairobi
Lesotho	Maseru
Liberia	Monrovia
Libya	Tripoli
Madagascar	Antananarivo
Malawi	Ligongwe
Mali	Bamako
Mauritania	Nouakchott
Mauritius	Port Louis
Morocco	Rabat
Mozambique	Maputo
Nambia	Windhoek
Niger	Niamey
Nigeria	Abuja
Reunion	St. Denis
Rwanda	Kigali
St. Helena	Jamestown
Sao Tome and Principe	Sao Tome
Senegal	Dakar
Seychelles	Victoria
Sierra Leone	Freetown
Somalia	Mogadishu
South Africa	Pretoria
Sudan	Khartoum
Swaziland	Mbabane
Tanzania	Dar es Salaam
Togo	Lome
Tunisia	Tunis
Uganda	Kampala
Western Sahara	El Aaiun
Zaire	Kinshasa
Zambia	Lusaka
Zimbabwe	Harare

Asia

Country	Capital	Country	Capital
Afghanistan	Kabul	Macao	Macao
Bahrain	Manama	Malaysia	Kuala Lumpur
Bangladesh	Dhaka	Maldives	Male
Bhutan	Thimphu	Mongolia	Ulaanbaatar
Brunei	Bandar Seri Begawan	Myanmar	Naypyidaw
Cambodia	Phnom Penh	Nepal	Kathmandu
China	Beijing	Oman	Muscat
Cyprus	Nicosia	Pakistan	Islamabad
Hong Kong	Victoria	Philippines	Manila
India	New Delhi	Qatar	Doha
Indonesia	Jakarta	Saudi Arabia	Riyadh
Iran	Tehran	Singapore	Singapore
Iraq	Baghdad	Sri Lanka	Colombo
Israel	Jerusalem	Syria	Damascus
Japan	Tokyo	Taiwan	Taipei
Jordan	Amman	Tajikistan	Dushanbe
Kazakhstan	Alma-Ata	Thailand	Bangkok
Korea, North	Pyongyang	Turkey	Ankara
Korea, South	Seoul	Turkmenistan	Ashkhabad
Kuwait	Kuwait City	United Arab Emirates	Abu Dhabi
Kyrgyzstan	Bishkek	Uzbekistan	Tashkent
Laos	Vientiane	Vietnam	Hanoi
Lebanon	Beirut	Yemen	Sana'a

Oceania

Country	Capital
American Samoa	Pago Pago
Australia	Canberra
Christmas Island	—
Cocos Islands	West Island
Cook Islands	Rarotonga Island
Fiji	Suva
French Polynesia	Papeete
Guam	Agana
Kribati	Bairiki
Marshall Islands	Dalap-Ukiga-Darrit
Micronesia, Federated States of	Palikir
Nauru	Yaren
New Caldonia	Noumea
New Zealand	Wellington
Niue	Alofi
Norfolk Island	Kingston
Northern Mariana Islands	Saipan
Palau	Korror
Papua New Guinea	Port Moresby
Pitcairn Island	Adamstown
Solomon Islands	Honaira
Tasmania	Hobart
Tokelau	—
Tonga	Nuku'alofa
Tuvalu	Funafuti
Vanuatu	Vila
Wallis and Futuna Islands	Mata-Utu

World Geography Skills Test

Match the letters on the map to the correct geographic features.

_____ 1. peninsula

_____ 2. gulf

_____ 3. delta

_____ 4. island

_____ 5. bay

_____ 6. source of river

_____ 7. channel

_____ 8. river

_____ 9. cape

_____ 10. strait

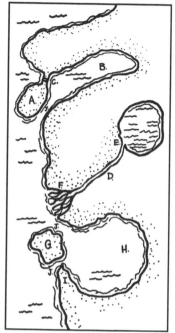

Questions 11–30 give descriptions or definitions of geographic features. Write the letter of the correct feature that matches each definition.

11. _____ line of latitude at 23.5° N latitude
12. _____ body of land nearly surrounded by water
13. _____ a narrow strip of land, bordered by water, connecting 2 larger bodies of land
14. _____ a narrow waterway connecting 2 larger bodies of water
15. _____ a large chain of islands
16. _____ a large, high, flat landform
17. _____ east-west lines on a map that show distance from the equator
18. _____ the starting line for measuring longitude
19. _____ line of latitude at 23.5° S latitude
20. _____ forms at the mouth of a river from soil deposits
21. _____ north-south lines on a map that show distance from the Prime Meridian
22. _____ imaginary line halfway around the globe from the Prime Meridian
23. _____ beginning of river or stream
24. _____ ring-shaped coral island or string of islands surrounding a lagoon
25. _____ river or stream that flows into a larger river or stream

26. _____ part of ocean or sea that extends into the land
27. _____ place where river empties into another body of water
28. _____ projecting part of a coastline that extends into an ocean, sea, or gulf
29. _____ line of latitude at 0°.
30. _____ place in desert made fertile by a steady supply of water

a lines of latitude	l tributary
b lines of longitude	m source
c archipelago	n mouth
d plateau	o oasis
e delta	p equator
f isthmus	q gulf
g peninsula	r International Date Line
h strait	s cape
i Prime Meridian	t atoll
j Tropic of Capricorn	
k Tropic of Cancer	

Name _____

Identify the continents and bodies of water shown on the map below.

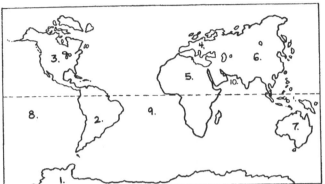

31. Continent # 1 _____
32. Continent # 2 _____
33. Continent # 3 _____
34. Continent # 4 _____
35. Continent # 5 _____
36. Continent # 6 _____
37. Continent # 7 _____
38. Body of Water # 8 _____
39. Body of Water # 9 _____
40. Body of Water # 10 _____

41. Which hemisphere is shown in **Figure A**?

_____

42. Which hemisphere is shown in **Figure B**?

_____

A   B

For Questions 43-50, write the letter of the world region that matches the description.

a Pacific	_____ 43. Thousands of islands, the world's smallest continent, and ocean-influenced climates
b Latin America	_____ 44. North American region stretching from the tropic of Cancer to the Arctic Ocean
c Russia & Eastern Europe	_____ 45. The world's largest country and many neighboring countries; many recent changes in political divisions
d Western Europe	_____ 46. A land of dry deserts, bridging two continents
e Sub-Saharan Africa	_____ 47. Mostly south of the equator; a land of high mountains and rain forests, home to the patagonia and the Panama Canal
f USA & Canada	_____ 48. Vast grasslands, tropical forests spanning from the tropic of Cancer south below the tropic of Capricorn
g Middle East & North Africa	_____ 49. Heavily populated with many small countries, the smallest region, loaded with peninsulas
h Southern & Eastern Asia	_____ 50. A region that holds a huge continent, most of the world's people; rich river valleys, the world's highest mountains and many islands

Name _____

For questions 51-56, write the number from
the map to the right that shows the location
of each of the bodies of water.

51. _____ Amazon River

52. _____ Gulf of Mexico

53. _____ Lake Superior

54. _____ Hudson Bay

55. _____ Caribbean Sea

56. _____ Mississippi River

For questions 57-79, write the correct letter
or letters of the answer in the blank

57. _____ Which of the following is not in the Pacific region of the world?
   a. Indonesia b. India c. Philippines d. Australia

58. _____ Which countries are in Western Europe?
   e. Denmark f. Spain g. Finland h. France i. all of these

59. _____ Which states are in the mountain region of the U.S.?
   a. Oregon & Idaho b. Utah & Arizona c. Montana & Kansas d. New Mexico & Nebraska

60. _____ Which country is not in Eastern Europe?
   e. Belgium f. Belarus g. Croatia h. Latvia i. Hungary

61. _____ Which are Canadian provinces?
   a. Nova Scotia b. Greenland c. Prince Edward Island d. Quebec e. Ontario

62. _____ Which African country is farther south than Egypt?
   f. Kenya g. Algeria h. Tunisia i. Morocco

63. _____ Saudi Arabia, Israel, Syria, Jordan, and Iran are in what world region?
   a. Asia b. Eastern Europe c. Western Europe d. Middle East & North Africa

64. _____ Which states are in the southern region of the U.S.?
   e. Arkansas f. Ohio g. Virginia h. North Carolina i. Kansas

65. _____ Which countries are not in sub-Saharan Africa?
   a. Zaire b. Congo c. Chad d. Morocco e. Botswana f. South Africa g. Algeria

66. _____ Which country is not in the Middle East?
   h. Iraq i. Iran j. Cyprus k. Albania l. Jordan

67. _____ Which type of climate could not be found along the equator?
   a. desert b. mountain c. polar d. tropical

68. _____ Which country is not in Asia?
   e. Mongolia f. Vietnam g. Thailand h. Singapore i. Greece j. Laos

69. _____ Which countries are in the Pacific region?
   a. South Korea b. Nepal c. Fiji d. New Zealand e. Taiwan

70. _____ Which state is not in the North Central Region of the U.S.?
   f. North Dakota g. Missouri h. Indiana i. Kentucky j. Ohio k. Michigan

71. _____ Mexico, Canada, Bolivia, Costa Rica, and Honduras are all in which hemisphere?
   a. Northern b. Southern c. Eastern d. Western

72. _____ Which is not a Central American country?
   e. Botswana f. Costa Rica g. Belize h. Guatemala i. Honduras

Name _____

73. _____ Which country is farther south in latitude?
        a. India b. South Africa c. Venezuela d. Mexico

74. _____ The large island off the southeast coast of Africa is
        e. South Korea f. New Zealand g. Cuba h. Madagascar i. Ireland

75. _____ Which countries are in southeast Asia?
        a. Laos b. Afghanistan c. Oman d. Cambodia e. Vietnam

76. _____ Which countries are on the equator?
        f. India g. Australia h. Brazil i. Chile j. Egypt

77. _____ Which countries are in Eastern Europe?
        a. Belarus b. Azerbaijan c. Estonia d. Ukraine e. All of these

78. _____ Which of these are not in the Pacific Region of the U.S.?
        f. Denver, CO g. Columbia River h. San Francisco, CA i. Pacific Ocean j. Seattle, WA

79. _____ Which is the world's largest country in area?
        a. China b. Russia c. U.S. d. India e. Canada

For questions 80-86, write the name that gives the answer.

80. the world's largest ocean

    _____

81. the world's longest river

    _____

82. the world's tallest mountain

    _____

83. the world's largest desert

    _____

84. the starting place for measuring latitude

    _____

85. the least inhabited continent

    _____

86. the largest state in the U.S.

    _____

For 91-100, write the letter of the country that matches each city.

91. _____	Paris	a	Peru
92. _____	Tokyo	b	Spain
93. _____	Toronto	c	Russia
94. _____	Rio de Janerio	d	Egypt
95. _____	Cairo	e	Poland
96. _____	Warsaw	f	France
97. _____	Amsterdam	g	China
98. _____	Moscow	h	Brazil
99. _____	Beijing	i	Netherlands
100. _____	Barcelona	j	Canada
		k	Japan
		l	Cuba
		m	Germany

Use the map below to answer questions 87-90.

87. Syria, Jordan, Turkey, and Iraq lie mostly between which two lines of longitude? _____

    _____

88. What body of water lies mostly between 15° and 30° N latitude?

    _____

89. What country is located at about 38°-55° E longitude and 13°-20° N latitude?

    _____

90. What country spreads from about 35°–55° E longitude?

    _____

Name _____

Skills Test Answer Key

1. A	35. Africa	69. c, d
2. H	36. Asia	70. i
3. F	37. Australia	71. d
4. G	38. Pacific Ocean	72. e
5. B	39. Atlantic Ocean	73. c
6. E	40. Arctic Ocean	74. h
7. C	41. Northern Hemisphere	75. a, d, e
8. D	42. Eastern Hemisphere	76. f, h
9. I	43. a	77. e
10. J	44. f	78. f
11. k	45. c	79. b
12. g	46. g	80. Pacific
13. f	47. b	81. Nile
14. h	48. e	82. Mt. Everest
15. c	49. d	83. Sahara
16. d	50. h	84. equator
17. a	51. 5	85. Antarctica
18. i	52. 3	86. Alaska
19. j	53. 6	87. 30°– 45°
20. e	54. 1	88. Red Sea
21. b	55. 4	89. Yemen
22. r	56. 2	90. Saudi Arabia
23. m	57. b	91. f
24. t	58. i	92. k
25. l	59. b	93. j
26. q	60. e	94. h
27. n	61. a, c, d, e	95. d
28. s	62. f	96. e
29. P	63. d	97. i
30. o	64. e, g, h	98. c
31. Antarctica	65. d, g	99. g
32. South America	66. k	100. b
33. North America	67. c	
34. Europe	68. i	

Answers

I. 1. archipelago
   2. fiord
   3. peak
   4. mountain
   5. mountain range
   6. foothills
   7. hill
   8. cliff
   9. volcano
   10. tundra
   11. canyon
   12. ocean
   13. iceberg
   14. glacier
   15. bay
   16. lake
   17. cape
   18. sound
   19. peninsula
   20. prairie
   21. dune
   22. beach
   23. river
   24. mouth
   25. delta
   26. plateau
   27. mesa
   28. butte
   29. plain
   30. valley
   31. swamp
   32. island
   33. isthmus
   34. atoll
   35. reef
   36. lagoon
   37. sea
   38. channel
   39. gulf
   40. strait
   41. port or harbor
   42. waterfall
   43. desert
   44. jungle

II. Allow answers to vary slightly from these definitions:

archipelago: a chain of islands
lake: a body of water completely surrounded by land
mountain range: a chain of mountains
bay: part of an ocean, sea, or lake that extends into the land
ocean: one of the earth's largest bodies of water
cape: a projecting part of a coastline that extends into an ocean, sea, gulf, bay, or lake
peak: the pointed top of a mountain
desert: a very dry area where vegetation is limited
river: a large stream of water that flows across land and usually empties into a lake or ocean
glacier: a large sheet of ice that moves slowly over some land surface
sea: a large body of water partly or entirely surrounded by land
gulf: part of an ocean or sea that extends into the land
strait: a narrow waterway connecting two larger bodies of water
isthmus: a narrow strip of land, bordered by water that connects two larger bodies of land
volcano: an opening in the earth through whch lava, rock, gases, or ash are forced out
waterfall: a flow of water falling from a high place to a lower place

Examples of the features will vary. Check to make sure students have included no more than 2 from any one world region.

Page 12

Maps will vary.

Check to see that all continent and major bodies of water are in relatively accurate size and location.

Page 13

1. Northern	Asia, N. America, S. America, Europe, Asia
Southern	Asia, Australia, Antarctica, S. America, Africa
Eastern	Europe, Africa, Asia, Australia, Antarctica
Western	N. America, S. America, Antarctica, Asia

2. Western & Northern
3-4. Look at student examples to see that they are correct.
5. N. America, S. America
6. S. America
7. Antarctica, Asia
8. Antarctica, Australia
9. Asia
10. Arctic Ocean
11. N. America, Europe
12. All 4
13. N. America
14. Australia
15. Indian

Page 14

Check student maps for accuracy.

Page 15

Trip plans will vary.

Check to see that students have included all required elements in each week's plan.

Page 16-17

1. 1. Mexico
   2. Guatemala
   3. Belize
   4. Honduras
   5. El Salvador
   6. Nicaragua
   7. Costa Rica
   8. Panama
   9. Cuba
   10. Haiti
   11. Dominican Republic
   12. Puerto Rico
   13. Jamaica
   14. Venezuela
   15. Colombia
   16. Ecuador
   17. Peru
   18. Brazil
   19. Guyana
   20. Suriname
   21. French Guiana
   22. Chile
   23. Bolivia
   24. Paraguay
   25. Uruguay
   26. Argentina

1-3. See map.
4. 22,834 feet or 6960 m
5. See map.
6. See map; Argentina
7. See map; Venezuela
8. See map; grassland plains of central Argentina
9. Yucatan
10. Patagonia
11. Chile, Bolivia, Peru, Ecuador, Colombia
12. Yes; the Andes Mountains run through this country—they are high enough for snow.
13. It is the narrowest point of land between the 2 oceans.
14. Ecuador, Colombia, Brazil
15. See map; Falkland Islands
16. See map; Galapagos Islands

Page 18

1. Hudson Bay
2. St. Lawrence River
3. Rocky Mountains
4. Mississippi-Missouri River
5. Lake Superior
6. Arctic Ocean
7. Alaska
8. Gulf of Mexico
9. Appalachian Mountains
10. Aleutian Islands
11. Death Valley
12. Niagara Falls
13. Columbia River
14. Quebec
15. Michigan
16. Arizona
17. Florida
18. Hawaii

19. Rio Grande River
20. MacKenzie River

Page 19

These are the countries to locate on the puzzle:

Andorra	Luxembourg
Austria	Monaco
Belgium	Netherlands
Denmark	Norway
England	Portugal
Finland	San Marino
France	Scotland
Germany	Spain
Greece	Sweden
Iceland	Switzerland
Ireland	Vatican City
Italy	Wales
Liechtenstein	

Page 20-21

1. Ural
2-5 See map.
6. Caucasus, Pamir
7-9. See map.
10. Georgia, Azerbaijan, Kazakhstan, Mongolia, China, North Korea
11. Norway, Finland, Estonia, Latvia, Belarus
12. 4800 miles or 7700 k—answers may vary depending on source.

Page 22

1. Greece, Albania
2. Slovenia, Croatia, Montenegro, Albania, Greece, Bosnia and Herzegovina
3. Poland, Latvia, Estonia, Lithuania
4. Black Sea
5. Czech Republic & Slovakia
6. Belarus or Russia
7. Bulgaria, Macedonia, Albania
8. Hungary and Germany
9. Moldova
10. Solvenia, Croatia, Bosnia and Hercegovina, Serbia, Montenegro, Macedonia
11. Ionian
12. yes

Page 23

ACROSS	DOWN
2. Cyprus	1. Turkey
6. Saudia Arabia	3. Morocco
9. Libya	4. Lebanon
10. Iraq	5. Bahrain
11. Red Sea	7. Israel
13. Jordan	8. Algeria
15. Syria	10. Iran
16. Kuwait	12. Eqypt
	14. Oman

Page 24

Students need only one answer for each other than the letter.

1. B Egypt, Sudan
2. C Zaire
3. H Tanzania
4. F Tanzania, Uganda
5. N Mozambique, Tanzania, Kenya, Ethiopia
6. E Morocco, Algeria, Mali, Libya, Egypt, Sudan, Chad, Niger, Mauritania
7. O Mali, Niger, Senegal, Chad, Sudan, Maritania
8. M Ghana, Togo, Nigeria, Cameroon, Gabon, Equatorial Guinea, Benin
9. D Madagascar
10. I Morocco, Libya, Egypt, Algeria, Tunisia
11. A Botswana
12. G Morocco, Algeria, Tunisia
13. J Somalia
14. P Guinea, Sierra Leone, Ivory Coast, Ghana, Benin, Togo, Nigeria, Cameroon, Chad, Sudan, Ethiopia, Zaire, Rwanda, Kenya, Uganda, Central African Republic
15. L South Africa
16. K Mozambique or Madagascar

Page 25

I. Students need write only one country for each letter.

C China, Cambodia
I India
L Laos
M Mongolia
P Pakistan, Philippines
N Nepal, North Korea
S Sri Lanka, South Korea
T Thailand, Taiwan
A Afghanistan
J Japan
B Burma, Bangladesh
V Vietnam
R Russia

II.
1. Mt. Everest
2. monsoons
3. Pamir Knot
4. Chang Jiang
5. Gobi
6. paddies
7. Lake Baikal
8. Himalaya
9. Arctic tundra
10. rain forest
11. Indian subcontinent; India
12. The Philippines

Page 26

Australia-New Zealand

Interior is a desert called Outback
Mostly dry except for outer rims
Colonized by British convicts
Discovery of gold sped settlement
Famous underwater wonderland
World's smallest continent
Center of literature, film, and music

Antarctica

Land of glaciers
All but 2% covered with ice
Generally has a polar ice cap climate
Has no permanent settlements
Exploration undertaken in late 1800s
Loaded with icebergs and glaciers

Oceania

Mostly subtropical climate
Missionaries promoted European settlement
Comprised of 3 major island groups
Polynesia, Micronesia, Melanesia
Known for many volcanoes
Includes Tahiti, Easter Island, Figi, Papua New Guinea
Scene of bloody fighting during WWII
Islands made of coral
Early societies based on fishing lifestyles

Page 27

1-10. Answers will vary.
11. Arctic Ocean & Atlantic Ocean; Pacific Ocean and Southern Ocean
12. Robert E. Peary; Roald Amundsen
13. 1909; 1911
14. Answers will vary.
(No polar bears at South Pole; no penguins at North Pole)

Page 28

1. China, U.S., Russia
2. Botswana, Zaire
3. Brazil
4. corn, aluminum
5. wheat, rice, tobacco, fish, potatoes, corn, cattle, coal, iron ore, zinc, gold
6. wheat, potatoes, crude oil, natural gas, coal, iron ore, copper, aluminum, diamonds
7. Brazil, Argentina
8. Brazil, Australia
9. Russia, U.S.
10. rice

Page 29

1. Russia
2. India
3. India
4. Approx. 3,020,000,000
5. Approx. 4,050,000,000

6. China and India
7. Approx. 240 million
8. Russia
9. China, India, Pakistan
10. China, India

Page 30
1. Denver . . . . in California
2. London . . . . . . on European continent
3. Mexico City . . . . . . in South America
4. Tokyo . . . . in China
5. Toronto . . . . in U.S.
6. Bucharest . . . . in Africa
7. Montevideo. . . . . in Brazil
8. Auckland . . . . in Australia
9. Manila . . . . . . in Western Hemisphere
10. Caracas . . . . in Eastern Europe
11. Athens. . . . . in Southeast Asia
12. Helsinki . . . . in Russia
13. Amsterdam . . . . in British Isles
14. Ankara. . . . . in Central America;
all capitals
15. Nice . . . . in Middle East
16. Quito . . . . in North America
17. New York City . . . . . all capital cities
18. Miami. . . . . sites of modern
Olympic summer games

Page 31
ACROSS
1. Asia
9. Hood
12. Panama
13. English Channel
16. Australia
17. Savanna
DOWN
1. Sinai
2. Vincent Massif
3. Madagascar
4. Grand Canyon
5. Kalahari
6. Indonesia
8. Amazon
10. Himalayas
11. Pyrenees
14. Ural
15. Alps

Page 32
1. Pacific
2. Kentucky; Mammoth
3. Malaysia; Petronas Towers
4. North Africa; 3,500,000 sq miles
5. Antarctica
6. Caspian Sea
7. South China: Eastern
8. in Canada
9. International Falls, Minnesota
10. Australia
11. Amazon; South America
12. Superior, Michigan

13. Angel; Venezuela
14. Greenland; Atlantic/Arctic
15. Yosemite
16. no; Alaska
17. Gulf of Mexico
18. Rhode Island
19. Arizona
20. Vatican City
21. Africa
22. Waimangu
23. Crater Lake

Page 33
24. Egypt
25. India
26. Lake Baikal; Russia
27. Japan; 33.49 miles
28. Mt. Guallatiri; Chile
29. Verrazano Narrows; mouth of Hudson River
30. Chicago
31. Australia
32. Nepal; Tibet
33. K-2; Kashmir-China
34. Nordvest
35. Vatican City
36. Marianas Trench
37. Tokyo-Yokohama, Japan
38. Everglades; Florida
39. Mt. Ranier, Washington
40. Dead Sea, Israel
41. Canada
42. Russia
43. New York City
44. Rotterdam, Netherlands
45. St. Augustine, Florida, founded in 1565
46. Nunathloogagamiutbingoi Dunes, Alaska

Page 34
1. Arctic Ocean
2. Bay of Bengal
3. Adriatic Sea
4. English Channel
5. Sea of Japan
6. Persian Gulf
7. Amazon River
8. Bering Sea
9. Atlantic Ocean
10. Indian Ocean
11. James Bay
12. Crater Lake
13. Red Sea
14. Mediterranean Sea
15. Gulf of Mexico
16. Strait of Mala
17. Pacific Ocean
18. Mississippi-Missouri
19. Strait of Gibralter

Page 35
1. a swim suit; coral; Australia
2. 167 feet; U.S. or Canada

3. 5300; Arizona
4. high salt content prohibits most life; between Israel and Jordan
5. Zambezi River; 355 feet
6. 29,023 feet; Nepal or China
7. floating glacier; Antarctica; about 1000 feet
8. China
9. Answers will vary (Ex: Oxford University, Windsor Castle, London, Tower of London, Hampton Court, English Parliament; England).
10. vast semiarid plateau in South America (Argentina); sheep
11. huge deep bay filled with icebergs; North Atlantic Ocean off Greenland
12. world's largest high lake; Andes Mountains between Peru and Bolivia

Pages 36-37
1. no
2. yes
3. no
4. no
5. no
6. yes
7. yes
8. no
9. no
10. no
11. yes
12. no
13. yes
14. no
15. yes
16. no

Page 38
A: 9—Statue of Liberty
B: 4—Taj Mahal
C: 1—Great Pyramid
D: 12—Stonehenge
E: 3—Great Wall of China
F: 2—Parthenon
G: 10—London Bridge
H: 5—Eiffel Tower
I: 7—Notre Dame
J: 11—Colosseum
K: 6—Easter Island
L: 8—Leaning Tower of Pisa

Page 39
1. Arizona
2. Massachusetts
3. Arkansas
4. North Dakota
5. Nova Scotia
6. Mississippi
7. Br. Columbia
8. NW Territory
9. Ohio
10. California
11. New Brunswick
12. Pennsylvania
13. Illinois
14. New Hampshire
15. Prince Edward
16. Iowa
17. New Jersey
18. Rhode Island

19. Kansas
20. Newfoundland
21. South Carolina
22. North Carolina
23. Louisiana
24. Yukon Territory

Pages 40-41

1. Answers will vary.
2. Atlantic; Gulf of Mexico
3. Southern
4. Northeast
5. North Central
6. North Central
7. Pacific
8. South or North Central
9. St. Paul, Baton Rouge; North Central, Southern
10. Mountain
11. Michigan
12. Mountain
13. Maine
14. Washington, Oregon, or California
15. West Virginia

Page 42

A. Albany
B. San Antonio
C. OK
D. New Orleans
E. Vancouver
F. OK
G. Seattle
H. Tulsa
I. Detroit
J. Savannah
K. Philadelphia
L. Knoxville
M. Montreal
N. OK
O. Charleston
P. Anchorage
Q. OK
R. Birmingham
S. OK
T. Boise
U. OK
V. Salt Lake City
W. OK

Page 43

1. Examine student diagrams to see that they have done this correctly.
2. 50° E
3. Asia
4. 140° E
5. Europe, Africa, and Asia
6. Every line of longitude passes through the equator.

Page 44

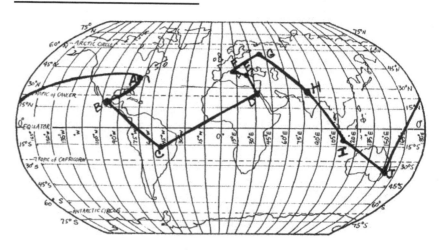

Page 45

1. North on 89, west on 412 about 15 miles
2. By water about 40 miles; yes, at least one night
3. Chesterfield
4. About 40 miles
5. Answers will vary.

Page 46

Maps, keys, and information will vary.

Pages 47-48

1. 24
2. 15
3. 7:00 A.M.
4. Tuesday, 6:00 A.M.
5. 1:00 P.M.
6. 7:00 P.M.
7. 11:00 P.M.
8. Tuesday, 4:00 P.M.
9. Friday, 1:00 A.M.
10. 9:00 A.M.
11. Sunday, 9:00 P.M.